The Seriously Weird History

of Australia

VOL 2

BY

DOUG BRADBY

ILLUSTRATIONS BY CARSON ELLIS

Inquiries should be made to:
Seaview Press
PO Box 7339
West Lakes, South Australia 5021
Telephone 08 8242 0666; fax 08 8242 0333
E-mail: seaview@seaviewpress.com.au
Web site: http://www.seaviewpress.com.au

Printed by:
Salmat Document Management Solutions Pty Limited
11 James Congdon Drive, Mile End, South Australia 5031.

National Library of Australia Cataloguing-in-Publication entry

Author: Bradby, Doug. (Douglas Neil), 1948-

Title: The seriously weird history of Australia
                   (vol. 2) / Doug Bradby.

ISBN: 9781740085045 (pbk.)

Notes: Bibliography.

Target Audience: For all ages

Subjects: Australia--History.

Dewey Number: 994

For my wife, Julie,

who, after I had procrastinated on this book for years,
caused me 'to get a move on',
by asking if I intended to publish the book posthumously.

FOREWORD

Those who cannot remember the past are condemned to repeat it. How correct the 19th century Spanish philosopher, George Santayana, was when he penned these now-famous words. But how to foster an enduring interest in remembering the past and how to engender a lifelong love of history: that is the challenge!

Written by a consummate teacher, with a zest for history and with a passion for nurturing critical thinking skills in his students, both young and old, here, in Volume 2 of The Seriously Weird History of Australia, is a resource of inestimable value, most especially for teachers at primary and secondary levels.

The proverbial men and women of Australia will relish reading it, for the sheer love of the subject matter. But teachers will find it a wellspring of fascinating stories and bite-sized snippets that will tantalize their students and provide food for thought and discussion in their classrooms. There are not a lot of answers here – but, rather, a lot of thought-provoking stories, fascinating cameos, intriguing vignettes, and teasing questions. Enjoy!

Associate Professor Anne Hunt OAM
Rector
Australian Catholic University
Ballarat Campus

The story so far …

In our past exciting century, a small group of convicts, soldiers, explorers and miners had accidentally, unexpectedly, and inexplicably succeeded. They had produced a nation; a free, democratic, prosperous nation.

What lay ahead for them? Did they live happily ever after as they hoped, or did life provide them with the usual rollercoaster ride of success and failure? Of course it did.

How did they cope with the unexpected? Did hard times harden them? Did wars destroy them? Did prosperity make them complacent and lazy? Volume 2 of *The Seriously Weird History of Australia* examines these Australia-shattering, world-shattering questions.

Volume 2 also asks intriguing, trivial questions. Was Lilly Langtry amusing? What role did Duffy play in World War I? Did Bertie Hinkler kidnap dogs? Where is Koepanger? Who is the Rawleigh's man?

Volume 2 contains more world history than Volume 1. In the 19th century, 'the tyranny of distance' ensured Australia was largely self-contained. Australia just got on with the job of developing the country.

In the 20th century, 'distant tyrannies' ensured Australia was impacted upon by global economic and political pressures. Australia now had to accept it was not 'an island unto itself alone'. For good or evil, I am, you are, we are, Australians, connected to the world.

Read on and continue to learn and laugh and wonder and ponder about our Australian story.

CONTENTS

'HISTORY IS JUST ONE DAMNED DECADE AFTER ANOTHER'.

HENRY FORD (MISQUOTED)

The Edwardian Age. The First 'Decade.' 1901-1913.

KING EDWARD. THE KING NOT THE POTATO.

Queen Victoria died within a month of the birth of the new nation and while Victoria may not have been amused very often, the new monarch, King Edward VII, certainly was amused, particularly by Lillie Langtry. The Victorian Age was over; now we had a new century, a new nation, a new monarch, a new attitude, a new age and a label to define this age, the Edwardian Age. What other labels could have been used? It could have been called 'The Foundation Years' or 'The Age of Optimism', or 'The Federation Age' which was certainly used by many to describe the lovely architecture of the time. Knowing the horror of what was coming in the next decade, 'Our Indian Summer' would be an accurate label.

The Edwardians, however, saw no clouds on the horizon, let alone a winter. The Edwardian Age it was and let us leave it at that and allow 'the Australian Edwardians' to enjoy their times and their optimistic plans for themselves and their country; for hope, optimism and a belief in progress abounded in 1901.

A New, Improved Britannia.

So from Jan 1st 1901, we were all Australians as well as being Victorians and Queenslanders and South Australians and New South Welshers or whatever they called themselves. At the same time as we were proud Tasmanians etc and proud Australians, we were also proud members of the British Empire, the empire upon which the sun never set. Did anyone suffer an identity crisis? Was anyone confused? Many Irish Australians were not that comfortable being an MBE (a member of the British Empire) but most Australians had no trouble with these layers of loyalties. They were British and they were Australians, as simple as that and they were going to create a New Britannia in the Antipodes.

Wrights and Wongs.

The founding fathers — there were no founding mothers apparently — set out to establish the foundations for the new country. The key question was, Who could be an Australian? 'Australia for the Australians', said *The Bulletin* but that merely begs the question of who would be allowed to migrate to Australia. As it was a British colony, obviously it was to be a country for the children of the mother country, so British people, the English, Scottish, Irish and Welsh, were welcome.

However, there was a problem. Indians, Africans and Chinese living in Hong Kong were all part of the British Empire. Could they pass through our ports with their British passports? We certainly needed them to populate, defend and develop the country, but they were not white. The new Australian Government, backed by the Australian people, firmly made up its mind; you could only enter Australia if you were white. This was just a little ridiculous as whites are not white at all. They are a sort of yellowy, pinky, browny, cream tan sort of colour.

It is worth pondering the question of why this White Australia Policy was so overwhelmingly popular in 1900. A meeting to oppose it could have been held in a red telephone box if one had been invented at the time. Some employers who wanted cheap labour would have attended. Some churchmen would also have attended as they remembered what they sang in Sunday school: 'Red and yellow, black and white/ all are equal in his sight/ Jesus loves the little children of the world/', all of them, equally. The slightly eccentric but often spot-on EW Cole, who produced wonderful children's books and sold them at Cole's Book Arcade, would have chaired the meeting. Cole argued that 'a permanent White Australia is a physical impossibility' as 'Australia lies in the tropics and semi-tropics, and consequently all her people must become more or less coloured'. (Cole 1902)

Against this small band would have been the vast majority of Australians. The working man, the Labor Party and the unions were worried about cheap labour undermining the Australian standard of living. The liberals, like Alfred Deakin, believed that 'Unity of race is an absolute essential to the unity of Australia', as it 'implies one inspired towards the same ideals'. (Cathcart and Darian Smith 2004) The new nation was not just a piece of geography, it was to be a collection of people with the same ideals, of democracy presumably. The assumption, the incredible assumption, was that only white people could be inspired by the ideal of democracy.

LIBERTY, EQUALITY, MATESHIP.

However, defining and implementing democracy was to prove far more complicated than they thought. Now, 100 years later, we are still sorting out the balance and tensions between how much diversity we can allow and how much unity we need. Must you believe in democracy to be an Australian? What if liberty leads to inequality? What if equality destroys liberty? Are there limits to mateship? Should we tolerate intolerance?

The British Government objected to the place of origin being used as the criterion to exclude people from Australia as 'it is contrary to the general conceptions of equality which have been the guiding principles of British rule throughout the Empire'. For a new country that saw itself as superior to the mother country in that it gave 'a fair go' to all its people, this was a very annoying point. How dare class-ridden Britain lecture us about what was right? And it was doubly annoying to be lectured by others on morality, when you suspected, secretly of course, that they could be right. Furthermore, Britain claimed that it would be 'peculiarly offensive to Japan' (Cathcart 2004), Britain's and therefore Australia's new ally in the Pacific.

Couldn't the Australian Government find a way to exclude these people without offending them? It was tricky, but a devious way was found and the government decided that 'non-white' people wanting to enter Australia had to pass a 50-word dictation test, usually in English. But if they knew English then the test would be administered in another language until they failed. So if they failed in Polish or Sanskrit, then obviously they would not be good citizens and would be refused entry to Australia. Some people worried that they might apply this dictation test to everyone in Australia, say, at the age of 14 in which case most Australians would have had to look for another country; one that didn't care about spelling.

NATURALLY AUSTRALIAN.

The Federal Government also ensured that all people who were born somewhere else but who wanted to become Australians, and who passed or by-passed the spelling test, were naturalised. Surely that can't be correct; the word must be nationalised. No, the word is naturalised. Were they suggesting, therefore, that if you were not Australian you were not natural? It has to be said, this is weird, arrogantly and offensively weird.

FREE TRADE VERSUS NEW PROTECTION.

The terms on which we would allow foreigners to sell their goods in Australia became the second hot issue. Follow this if you can. One of the key reasons why the states federated was to establish the whole of Australia as one huge unrestricted market, a huge continent-wide free trade zone. By eliminating taxes on interstate sales and by allowing producers to gain the economies of scale by producing more items, the price of goods would be lowered. This not only lowers prices and raises living standards, it also increases employment. Sounds good, I'm convinced. However one of the first things the founding fathers did was to make sure that goods coming into Australia were not free, but taxed. Presumably, this had the opposite effect; that is, the tax increased the prices of the goods and led to a lower standard of living.

This tax, a tariff, was called protection as it protected the local industry by increasing the price of foreign goods and 'encouraged' people to buy Australian-made, and this would develop Australian industries and increase employment in Australia. The politicians argued that to have a high standard of living AND employment, we needed free trade in Australia but protection from the rest of the world. Does this make sense? Were the policies contradictory? The states supported tariffs as they needed the revenue to support services such as education and roads. Workers supported tariffs to protect their jobs. Exporters, farmers and miners, however, worried that other countries might do the same as we were doing and tax Australian exports out of their markets. They also wanted to buy machinery as cheaply as possible so they were free traders. Who was right?

POVERTY IN HISTORY.

Anyway, who cares, this is just an obscure, complicated debate from the dim distant past. Well, no, it isn't actually, the wellbeing of billions of people is involved. It is one of the ongoing crucial debates in the world today. (And it doesn't matter if you read this ten years from 'today' the statement will still be true.) Ask yourself what is the most important thing that can be done to lift the world's poor out of poverty? What needs to be done to provide African people with decent education, health care, housing? Is free trade the answer? Protection? Fair trade? Aid? Population control? Development? Industrialisation? Globalisation?

Many countries, called first world countries, have already lifted the overwhelming majority of their people out of poverty. How did they do it? Britain was the first country to lift a substantial proportion of its people out of poverty. How did Britain do it? How did the USA lift the poor and huddled masses out of poverty? How did Japan lift its people out of poverty after World War II? How are China and India lifting their billions out of poverty today? Perhaps the study of history might provide some answers for Africa? What, study — useful?

In Australia in 1900 the protectionists such as Barton and Deakin won. Australia adopted protection, 'new protection' it was called as it came with strings attached. However, in the past 20 years we have reversed the decision and swung back to free trade. What will happen to Australia's standard of living if we adopt free trade? What will happen to employment in Australia? Were our ancestors right or are we right? Which policy is likely to produce the highest standard of living and the greatest number of jobs in Australia? Are we doing the right thing by the world's poor but the wrong thing by our own self-interest by lowering our tariffs? We will come back to this conundrum later in the century.

SHINE ON HARVESTER JUDGMENT.

The government was also keen to establish a society that enabled its citizens to live decently, at the normal standard of 'a human being living in a civilized society'. Companies, therefore, could not receive this new protection from cheap imports unless they paid a wage that allowed a family to live in a decent way in a civilized society. This was tested by Hugh Victor McKay, who applied for protection for his company, the Sunshine Harvester Company.

Justice Higgins calculated that the company was not passing on enough sunshine into the lives of its workers because it was not paying the 'basic wage', that is, a wage sufficient to support a basic standard of living. For the average male married with three children this basic wage was seven shillings a day (seventy cents in today's terms). Fortunately, seventy cents was worth more than seventy cents in those days. You know what I mean. In making his calculations, Justice Higgins did assume that the wife was a dependent and that 'marriage was the usual fate of an adult man', which makes marriage sound like a disease. Feminism, as we know it, was not that strong in 1907.

ONE GIANT LEAP FOR MANKIND. BACKWARDS.

Until 1900, Aboriginals, as British subjects, had enjoyed the right to vote in NSW, Victoria, Tasmania and South Australia. And even in Western Australia and Queensland they could vote if, like the Europeans, they met the property qualifications. However, in 1900 their right to vote was taken from them; not only could they not vote in federal elections, they could no longer vote in any state elections. They were disenfranchised! Richard O'Connor, a Minister in the Barton government, called this decision 'a monstrous thing', 'an unheard of piece of savagery'. (Hirst 2002) You had to be fair-skinned to get a fair go, apparently.

Most Australians at the time saw themselves as progressives, liberals, democrats, who were going to establish a society that was fairer and more advanced that anywhere else in the world and yet … *The Bulletin*, Australia's nationalistic magazine, was annoyed that Lord Beauchamp, the Governor of NSW, congratulated Australia for overcoming its 'birth stains', our convict past, yet *The Bulletin* made no mention of this particular stain created by ourselves at the moment of our birth as a nation.

Blokes and Votes, Sheilas and Suffrage.

When it came to the question of votes for women, the progressive views of the times reappeared. South Australian women had been voting since 1894 and it was agreed that they would keep this right to vote for the new Australian parliament. Therefore, to be fair, women in all the other states should have the right to vote as well. Indeed, virtually without debate or controversy, the vote, the suffrage as it was called, was extended to all women in Australia and in the election of 1903 women throughout the land, voted. One woman, Vida Goldstein, stood as a candidate but it was to be another forty years before a woman sat in federal parliament. Voting, by the way, was voluntary and 66 per cent volunteered in 1903 and the counting was done by the simple first-past-the-post system. Why are we now compelled by law to vote? Why do we now have a preference for the preference system?

A Fair Go for the Fair.

The parliament did introduce some valuable legislation with the introduction of old age and invalid pensions and the payment of maternity allowances. Who should get the credit? It's difficult to say, really as, although they had political parties at the time, the Free Traders, the Protectionists and the Australian Labor Party, they sort of played turnabout as to which party would form the government. Alfred Deakin was Prime Minister for much of the time and according to many historians he was a great Australian, just as great as Phar Lap and Sir Donald Bradman respectively, very respectively, but this sounds like an exaggeration to me. However, while Prime Minister, Deakin did write anonymously for an English newspaper in which he was critical of his own performance as Prime Minister; this proves nothing, but it's weird so it should be included in this book.

DEFENDING THE DEFENDABLE.

The other major concern was with defence, as there were fewer than four million Australians in 1901 and as they were so 'picky' about who they admitted into Australia, this number was hardly likely to grow very quickly. As for Britain's new alliance with Japan, this worried rather than reassured many Australians. The answer was to establish the Royal Australian Navy (RAN) which had a battle cruiser, three cruisers, three destroyers and two submarines by 1913. They RAN all over the place as a sort of sidekick to the British Navy. which did most of the wave ruling at that time because, in truth, Australia in 1900 was protected by the strongest power in the world, Britain and the whole British Empire. However, in 1907 the government decided to go for a conscript army rather than a professional army just in case extra protection was needed.

Anything else memorable happen at that time? The Bendigo–Melbourne train ploughed into the back of the Ballarat train at Sunshine, killing 44 people. The British gave us their bit of New

12

Guinea to look after in 1906 and the Commonwealth took over the Northern Territory from South Australia in 1910. Kalgoorlie finally got its water supply although it took a long time to arrive. It had to travel 550 kilometres from the Western Australian coast. There was a severe drought, the Federation Drought, from 1895–1902, which halved the sheep in Australia. Not each sheep of course, the total number of sheep were halved. You could drive a horse and cart across the Murray River at Swan Hill; no bridge required. The Darling River virtually ran dry, which is a strange way of saying that it didn't 'run' at all. That's it. Oh, and we did win our first Davis Cup in 1907.

The Edwardians 'had a stab at' the major issues of their time. Well, actually, they are some of the major issues of our time as well. We are still grappling with questions about population and migration and equity and development, defence and Aboriginal rights. Are we coming up with better answers?

P. S. ROMANS LESS NUMEROUS.

I know that thirteen years is not a decade because dec means ten. However, 1913 is the logical place to end chapter one as 1914 was a lot different from 1913 whereas 1911 was much the same as 1910. This can be proven and will be at the start of the next chapter. What I don't understand is why, if dec means ten, December is the 12th month of the year. While I am on this thought, why is October not the 8th month and September not the 7th month? Rearrange the months properly, will you? I am, however, positive that dec means ten as I recall the horribly fascinating story that the Romans would sometimes kill every tenth soldier in any of their own armies which displayed cowardice in battle, hence the word decimate. The soldiers were sorry the word wasn't kilamate but they couldn't kill a mate so it had to be decimate.

THE GREAT WAR

THE SECOND 'DECADE'.
1914-1919.

The Great War began on the fourth of August 1914 and that made 1914 totally different from 1913. Told you so. On June 29th John Simpson Kirkpatrick might have read about an Austrian Archduke being assassinated in a place called Sarejevo, but he probably missed that edition of the 'Back-of-Bourke Gazette'. Within a year, however, Simpson and over 8,000 of his Australian cobbers died heroically on the slopes of another place he had never heard of — Gelibolu to the Turks, Gallipoli to the Australians.

DOMINOES IMPACT ON OUR DOMINION.

What was the sequence of events that led to this terrible war? Why did the nations, Britain and Australia included, turn to war? The sequence of tragic events began when Archduke Franz Ferdinand of Austria was assassinated by a Serb so Austria used this to place demands on little Serbia, which obtained support from Russia, but this caused Austria to get support from Germany, which led Russia to seek French help, so Germany attacked France through Belgium, which brought Britain into the war, so obviously and automatically Australia and therefore Simpson were involved. Got that? Perhaps you should rewind it and see if you can explain the fall of each domino and then you will understand what caused World War I, the Great War. Good luck.

HURRAH! THE PEACE HAS ENDED.

So how did the people of Australia react to this horrifying development? It is my melancholy duty to inform you that they reacted with wild enthusiasm and the politicians endorsed this enthusiasm. Andrew Fisher, the Labor Prime Minister, promised to fight to 'the last man and the last shilling' and to the last man and the last wife and mother he was cheered. Incredible! How do you get people to volunteer to go to war and face death or mutilation? How do you get bank clerks and drapers and shearers and drovers and Australia's best fast bowler at the time to agree to fight for their country? How do you get mild, ordinary people to agree to kill for their country? Even more puzzling, how do you get their wives and mothers to urge them to enlist? In 1914 there was no need to apply legal compulsion, conscription, they volunteered in their hundreds of thousands. Weird, incredibly weird.

THE FIRST ANGRY SHOT.

The first Australian action occurred on the very first day of the war when a German ship, which was docked at Melbourne, tried to make a run for it through the heads at Port Phillip Bay and the guns of Port Nepean convinced it not to. The captured *SS Pfalz* was renamed *HMAT Boorara* and had a very adventurous war. It took part in the Gallipoli campaign when it carried Turkish POWs from the Dardanelles, was nearly sunk when it was rammed by one of our own ships, the French cruiser *Kleber*, and survived two torpedo attacks off the English coast, one at Whitby, Captain Cook's home port. Finally, in 1919 it was involved in the operation to bring the Aussie troops home to Australia.

ODD FELLOWS ATTACK ODDFELLOWS.

A bizarre tragedy did occur on Australian soil when just outside Broken Hill on January the 1st 1915 two 'Afghans', hiding behind an ice-cream cart flying the Turkish flag, opened fire on an open train of 1200 picnickers from the Order of Oddfellows and killed four people. After a three-hour battle the two men, a local butcher and the local ice-cream vendor, were killed. A mob then attacked and burnt down the German Club; close enough, they thought. Fortunately that ended the violence as police intervention stopped the mob from attacking the 'Afghan' camp outside Broken Hill.

FROM HANDORF TO AMBLESIDE, STEINFELD TO STONEFIELD, GERMAN SHEPHERD TO ALSATIAN.

There were also about 100,000 people of German ancestry in Australia when the war began, indeed approximately 10 per cent of South Australians had a German background. How did they respond to the call to defend the British Empire against Germany? They must have been slightly confused, lost even, as 69 places with German place names in South Australia had their name changed. German shepherd dogs suddenly became Alsatians after Alsace, a German state that was about to be returned to France. Pity the poor students in Alsace schools who were being taught in German. One day the teacher walked in and said, 'Now we learn in French.' Presumably he said, 'Maintenant, nous apprenons en Francais.' In Australia, German schools were closed and some public figures such as the mayor of Rainbow had to leave public office. I wonder how surprised the Aussie diggers would have been if they knew their beloved general, John Monash, but originally Monasch as his family was from Germany, wrote his letters home to his father in German.

KING GEORGE V. THE KING NOT THE FISH.

King George V himself must also have been confused as he began the war as George Saxe-Coburg-Gotha and ended it as George Windsor. By the way, Queen Elizabeth II has kept the name Windsor. George V must also have been confused by the fact that he was leading his Empire to war against the German King, Kaiser Wilhelm II, his cousin. Queen Victoria wouldn't have been amused either that her grandson, Kaiser Wilhelm II, was at war with her grandson, King George V. Pity the family didn't get on better, they may have been able to put a stop to this war between whole nations. Wars of old tended to be short, sharp affairs between professional armies so, as long as you kept out of their way, life was fairly normal for normal people. But wars between nations were different, appallingly different. Everyone was involved and therefore the number of casualties would not be in the hundreds, or in the thousands or even in the tens of thousands but in the millions: eight and a half million is a generally accepted figure of deaths in World War I.

THE ANZACS.

The Australian Imperial Force (AIF) was quickly recruited to defend Australia. It was sent to attack Turkey. No it wasn't a geographical mistake, it was an attempt to aid Russia, our weakening ally, to secure the Arabian oil fields and to eliminate Turkey from the war. You do know the stories of the heroic ANZACS at Gallipoli, surely? Simpson and Duffy his donkey, the morning attack at Anzac cove, the fight for Lone Pine, and the successful evacuation are all part of the Legend of the Anzacs. There were actually a number of Duffys as they kept getting shot. But why is it called the legend of the ANZACs? Isn't it true?

You must also know the Anzacs did not achieve their objective. It was to take another three years and one million men to defeat Turkey under Kemal Ataturk or Mustafa Kemal as he was known to the Anzacs and that involved the Australian Light Horse charge at Beersheba in which Tibby Cotter, the Brett Lee of his age, was killed. What would have happened if the Anzacs had won at Gallipoli? Would the war have been over by Christmas? Would Russia have avoided the communist revolution of 1917?

Would the slaughter of the Western Front have been avoided? Who knows but Who isn't telling.

A Back-to-the-Front War.

Meanwhile, the situation back in Europe just got worse. The problem was that it didn't matter how brave you were, you could not charge a machine gun; well, you could, but you would be slaughtered. At the battle of Fromelles in July 1916, for example, Australia suffered 5,533 casualties in 24 hours. On the Western Front both sides dug in and stayed in the trenches for the next four years trying to work out how to break the stalemate. Just how can we attack our enemies without all being wiped out in the attack? They tried mass attacks, massive bombardments, gas, tunneling, creeping barrages and finally the new inventions, planes, and tanks which were not tanks at all but mobile gun carriages.

General Ignorance.

The Australian General, Sir John Monash, was one of the few generals to make some headway with this problem as Monash's methods of attack involved intelligence as well as bravery. Most generals suffered from second-degree ignorance; they were ignorant of the fact that they were ignorant. In one incident, Monash ordered his troops to bomb the German lines every morning with one-third bombs, one third-smoke and one-third gas. The Germans knew that as you cannot charge into gas, there would be no Australian attack. On the day of the attack, however, the mixture was changed to one-half bombs and one-half smoke. When the smoke cleared, the Germans surfaced to find the Australians had quietly walked across no-man's land during the bombardment.

Support for the War, Wobbles.

Meanwhile the situation back in Australia was becoming less united. The International Workers of the World, IWW or 'Wobblies', threatened to burn Sydney unless the Editor of *Direct Action* was released from jail. The editor had urged 'capitalists, parsons, politicians, landlords and other stay-at-home-patriots' to enlist and he added, 'Workers, follow your masters.' (Crowley 1974) The Irish also wondered how it could be that we were fighting for the rights of small nations such as Serbia and Belgium, but not Ireland. Not only the human cost but the very purpose of the war was being called into question.

The Welsh Rabbit. First Course.

By 1917, the number of volunteers for the AIF was not sufficient to replace the casualties. One answer was to reduce the casualties but they decided instead to increase the number of 'volunteers'. Our Welsh-speaking Prime Minister, William Morris Hughes, explained to his British counterpart, Welsh-speaking David Lloyd-George, that Australia would introduce conscription. Hughes may have opted for conscription but his party, the Australian Labor Party, didn't. Neither did the nation, which narrowly voted no to two conscription referendums. The Australian Imperial Force was to remain a volunteer army.

A bitter fight ensued within the ALP and Billy Hughes ended up on the other side in Parliament but still Prime Minister as leader of the new Nationalist Party. Billy, 'the little digger', was a cartoonist's delight, small with big ears that only worked when it suited him. The cartoonist David Low produced a 'Billiwog' a doll which you 'Blow up with wind until the head expands, then release hole in face, whereupon Billy will emit loud noises until he goes flat. No war is complete without one'. (*The Billy Book* 1918) Low presented one to Hughes who was not amused and furiously tore it up, jumped on the pieces and accused Low of a low act.

WORK, WAR AND WOMEN.

Women entered the war as Edwardian ladies and ended the war as 'flappers' with skirts considerably shorter. Did the war 'cause' this change, which was not only a change in dress but also a change in attitude? Possibly, probably, perhaps. In other words, I think so but cannot prove it. Women's contribution to the paid workforce did increase from 24 per cent to 37 per cent but the increase was largely in traditional areas and at the end of the war the returned soldiers returned to their jobs and women returned to their traditional roles. Their active war work largely consisted of work for organizations such as the Red Cross, although they were very active in the temperance movement, which shut the pubs at six o'clock. This was seen as vital for the war effort and the pubs continued to shut at six for the next 50 years.

1918. CRISIS ON THE WESTERN FRONT.

What a year. Russia had collapsed and was out of the war, the French Army was mutinous and Germany was making one last attack as they feared being overwhelmed by the Americans who were about to arrive. There is one village in France, Villers-Bretonneux, which was saved by the Australians during this last German push of March 1918 which has the motto 'Remember the Australians' written at the front of the village school. But now the tide did turn and Australians played a crucial role in the turning at Hamel (July the 3rd) and on the 8th of August when the German line, the Hindenburg line, was finally broken when British, Canadian, French and Australian troops penetrated miles through the enemy lines. Germany accepted defeat and the guns ceased at 11 o'clock on the 11th day of the 11th month (November), 1918.

1919. ALL FINALLY QUIET ON THE WESTERN FRONT.

In many ways, 1919 was the crucial year for the world. After the war was over, after the battle was won, the victors met at

Versailles, just outside Paris and hammered out a treaty that was to abolish war, make the world safe for democracy and redraw the map of Europe with nation states and no empires or emperors. At least that was the hope of Woodrow Wilson, the American President and most of the war-weary world. As far as the French were concerned this was just bosh, rubbish. What they wanted was a treaty that said the Boche, the Germans, caused the war and therefore they must pay for all the damage they caused. As for the 'no empire' rule, that was only to apply to Germany and Austria, not to the empires of the winners.

Basically, the French won, the Treaty of Versailles was a tough treaty and clause 231 stated that Germany had to pay for all the damage, although it must be said it was nowhere near as tough as the treaty of Brest-Litovsk which the Germans had foistered on the defeated Russians in 1917. Reparations they were called and the new German government, a democrat one now that Wilhelm had fled to the Netherlands, had to accept the terms and start paying up. Seeds had been sown, but not seeds of democracy and prosperity, rather seeds of hatred and future trouble. The Australian cartoonist, Will Dyson, in his cartoon 'Peace and Future Cannon Fodder' published in 1919, asserted that this treaty would produce another war by 1940. (*The Cartoon History of Britain* 1971) How did he know? Correct, chillingly correct.

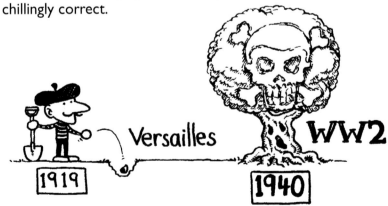

THE WELSH RABBIT. SECOND COURSE.

Australia's Prime Minister, Billy Hughes, played a very important part in the Peace Conference at Paris. At one stage he would not budge on a seemingly minor issue. 'Do you mean to tell me that you intend to hold up the whole civilized world?' said Woodrow Wilson, the American President. 'Yes. That's about the size of it,' said Hughes. 'But you only represent four million people!' said Wilson. 'I represent 60,000 dead,' was the crushing reply. Hughes was very good at standing up for Australia's interests as he saw them.

At times I wish he hadn't been as good at standing up for Australia's interests as he saw them. Wilson wanted to set up a League of Nations, so that in future nations could solve their differences by negotiation rather than war. The Japanese, who lost 415 killed fighting alongside us in World War I, moved for the inclusion of a racial equality clause. 'Fine,' said Hughes to the League of Nations but he insisted that the racial equality clause should be removed from the document as he thought it would threaten Australia's White Australia Policy. I wonder if Japan noticed who defeated the racial equality clause.

1919. Things Not So Quiet on the Eastern Front.

At the same time a new threat appeared, the red menace of Communism. Russia was turning into the Union of Soviet Socialist Republics (USSR) via a communist, red revolution. HMAS *Brisbane* and HMAS *Australia* were sent to the Black Sea, via the Red Sea, to fight for the Whites against the Reds. About 100–120 Australians also volunteered to fight with British forces and they were sent to the White Sea and two of them, Samuel Pearse and Arthur Sullivan, won Victoria Crosses for their bravery. Back in Australia some workers did not want to support White Australia so much as a Red Australia and with the support of some Russians in Brisbane these workers ran up the Red Flag and it took three days of fighting before they ran up the white flag. How times change. Today, if you expressed a choice for a red rather than a white you would, most likely be talking about wine, not politics.

At least we had peace and peace is usually coupled with prosperity. The decade of the 1920s promised much, but would it deliver?

THE DELIGHFUL DECADE OR THE DECADENT DECADE.

THE THIRD DECADE. 1920-1929

DELIGHTFUL OR DECADENT?

If this book was about the USA, then decadent would be the appropriate word. In the Roaring Twenties, the Americans introduced prohibition and it was the lack of legal alcohol that gave organized crime its chance. Prohibition led to gang warfare and the St Valentine's Day Massacre when seven members of 'Bugs' Moran's gang were machine-gunned by Al Capone and his men, 'Machine Gun' McGurn and 'Killer' Burke. Only their German shepherd guard dog, Highball, survived. The 1920s was also the decade of peak membership in the dreaded and dreadful Ku Klux Klan. But Charlie Chaplin and Buster Keaton and the Keystone Cops were not decadent. They were just good fun.

Australia had a sort of partial prohibition, the pubs shut at six o'clock and we had our criminals such as 'Squizzy' Taylor and 'Snowy' Cutmore who managed to kill each other in a shootout in Carlton, Melbourne. So the police force had work to do and they had to spend the next fifty years trying to stop Australians drinking after six, and gambling off racecourses, SP betting, starting price betting, it was called. They might as well have tried to wage war against the fly and the mosquito. However, delightful is the appropriate word for Australia, as, although the Twenties in Australia were far from perfect, it was a heaven of a lot better than the previous decade and what was coming up in the next two decades. Here is the evidence.

Peace, Imperfect Peace.

Australians greeted the announcement of peace just as enthusiastically as they had greeted the announcement of war in 1914. After years of war what the people wanted was fun and who could blame them? Mind you, initially there were some very serious difficulties. When the soldiers returned from the war they brought with them a strain of influenza that killed more Australians in 1919 than had died at Gallipoli. They had to resort to hanging a red flag at the gate of an infected house, a return to the Middle Ages. Passports were even issued to Victorians to cross into NSW but only after they had waited for four days at Albury to ensure that they were influenza-free.

Flapping About.

The Great War had been won and what they had won was liberty according to Billy Hughes, and the women in particular set out to enjoy it. The flappers, as they were called, went swimming in costumes that infuriated some men. Some other men were not infuriated. The flappers danced the Charleston, they went to the movies to see Rudolph Valentino and they even smoked in public. They were free and freedom means you can do any stupid thing you like, as long as you hurt no-one else.

Others were not so stupid. Edith Cowan became the first woman member of an Australian Parliament. Henry Handel Richardson completed her *Richard Mahony* trilogy. Ethel was actually her name on her birth certificate. Florence Gordon was instrumental in setting up the Country Women's Association (CWA). I wonder if she was impressed with Mr Bruxner MLA urging the new organization to fight for good roads, cheap power and at the same time to 'wage war against the fly and the mosquito'. (*Australia Through Time* 1997) Good advice, get on with it, I say.

Free they may have been but not equal. Miss Julia Flynn, an inspector of schools in Victoria, was refused permission to apply for the position of Chief Inspector. Not qualified enough? Not competent enough? No, three reasons were given. Firstly, she might have to talk about sanitary arrangements. Secondly, she might have to talk about s… Thirdly, as a woman it was felt she did not understand 'the needs of boys facing a life long vocation' which 'were far more complex than those of girls. Girls may start earning a wage but mostly they drop out after a few years and become housewives'. (*Australia Through Time* 1997) Strange how one can be absolutely factually correct, but absolutely wrong in terms of the argument.

Miss Flynn, educating children includes teaching them about S_X. And we feel that someone of your S_X, being the weaker S_X, may find it difficult to discuss S_X with children of the opposite S_X.

LIBERTY, EQUALITY, ELECTRICITY.

For most women, Monday was still washing day, Tuesday was ironing, Friday was shopping and Saturday was still baking day. Life was still a life of domestic drudgery but it was a drudgery reduced by electricity. Indeed, new inventions were beginning to alter the life of all Australians. By 1929, 300,000 owned a wireless, 100,000 electric irons were in use in Sydney and 20,000 had vacuum cleaners. 'Buy Hecla, its good' was the slogan of the Hecla company and as they sold 100,000 electric fires around Australia, it looks like a hec of a lot of people agreed with them. By 1930, 600,000 cars had been sold and some had actually been paid for although the new American idea of paying on the never-never was introduced at that time. Indeed, a whole lot of American ideas began to swim across the Pacific.

THOSE MAGNIFICENT PEOPLE IN THEIR DYING MACHINES.

It was aviation that Australians were really excited about in the twenties. We had heroes such as Charles Kingsford-Smith, Millicent Bryant, Maude Bonney and Bertie Hinkler who were ending Australia's isolation from its friends. They were also ending our isolation from our enemies but that is to jump or fly ahead in the story. When Bertie Hinkler flew into town the whole town turned up at the racecourse to welcome him. No, they were not lost, the racecourse was where he usually landed. An old bloke I know lost his dog in the huge crowd. His father told him that Bertie Hinkler stole it, but he can't prove it. Q.A.N.T.A.S. became QANTAS and began service with two planes capable of flying at the incredible speed of 100 kilometres per hour. Melbourne to Sydney in one day!

CSIR IS ORGANISED.

The Council for Scientific and Industrial Research (CSIR) was established in 1926 and one can see what was at the heart of this organization. They wanted to solve practical problems faced by industry. They made a brilliant start when the Commonwealth Prickly Pear Board introduced 20,000 eggs of the cactoblastis moth, which proceeded to blast the 24 million hectares of prickly pear off the face of Australia. That cactus was cactus. They also did great work controlling liver fluke in sheep and bitter-pit in apples. You haven't had any bitter-pits in apples lately, have you? There you go.

The work of the CSIR has continued for 80 productive years. In the 1930s they overcame coast disease in South Australian sheep by giving them a pellet of cobalt and copper. In the 1940s their work was largely hush-hush. It was largely radar-radar but Dr Doug Waterhouse became a hero when he developed a repellant to protect troops from malarial mosquitoes. Did the Country Women's Association play a role in this development? Myxomatosis was the big breakthrough in the 1950s when it wiped out 99 per cent of rabbits. MacFarlane Burnett, Ian Clunies-Ross and Frank Fenner were not wiped out when they injected themselves with myoxa to calm public fears that it caused human encephalitis. Progress produced permanent press pleating in the 1950s. The list of achievements is endless. Well, that is an exaggeration. The list of achievements is very long and is continuing to grow.

'OUR UNLEASHED SCUM.'

The Victorian police were not so busy on November the 5th 1923 when about one-third of them went on strike. The State Government responded with tough measures, the trams were stopped at six o'clock to try and stop people coming into the city. They also enrolled 1,500 special constables who tried to protect the shops in Bourke Street. They failed. In the pandemonium that followed, three men were killed and about 200 were treated at the Melbourne Hospital, mostly for 'cuts to the head', presumably obtained while looting shop windows. The newspapers certainly went to town on the striking police and the rioters with headings such as 'OUR UNLEASHED SCUM', 'SHAMELESS WOMEN', 'MACHINE GUNS READY', 'AUSTRALIA'S WORST EPISODE'. (*Famous News Pages* 1972)

As for the causes of the strike, one can only say that they were complex. What a cop-out! One should analyze why the cops went out. However, it is the consequences of there being no law and order which is the most interesting aspect of this event. How thin is the veil of civilization. Reminds me of *Lord of the Flies* and some *Simpsons* episodes when Springfield gets trashed. You don't know what you have got until it's gone. The rule of law is certainly a wonderful achievement.

CANBERRA TIME.

After 14 years, Parliament House in Canberra was ready and it was opened by the Duke of York, the future King George VI, the father of Queen Elizabeth, on May 10th 1927. About 35,000 people listened to Dame Nellie Melba sing. One Aboriginal arrived for the ceremony but a policeman led him away; he was not properly dressed apparently. Two other political developments are of interest. Compulsory voting was introduced for the 1925 federal election and the Upper House in Queensland was abolished. We have here one of the few examples of politicians voting themselves out of a job. Well done, Queensland, you should be in *The Guinness Book of Records*. The outhouse was still kept, however, for most Australians.

THE LOT OF NOT A LOT OF ABORIGINALS.

75,604 was the number of Aboriginals recorded in the 1921 census. 'A dying race' was a typical heading and the tone of the articles suggests sadness combined with smugness. A terrible embarrassment did not have to be addressed, it was just going to go away. Daisy Bates published her 'defeatist views' in *The Passing of the Aborigines.* An incredible woman, a Justice of the Peace, three times visited by royalty, who lived for 15 years with the Aboriginals of Ooldea, a permanent water hole on the trans-Australian railway. Her humanitarian and anthropological work 'remain the subject of sustained controversy.' How can humanitarian work be controversial?

One of the reasons that the Aboriginals were a dying race was that they were being killed. 'Police agree that W.A. Blacks were Massacred' is the heading in the newspaper in May 1927. 'Sixteen killed' says the article, 'between 11 and 100' says another article. A posse sent out to find one Aboriginal accused of murder had acted as a punitive expedition and had rounded up and shot all the Aboriginals they could find. The massacres continued for one week. It is unlikely that those responsible were ever held to account for this atrocity. As the Police Inspector said, the Minister of Religion who reported the murders, the Rev. Gribble, 'is so cordially hated that most men here will go to any measure to thwart his object.' (*Famous News Pages* 1972) What was his object — justice?

BEDS, BISCUITS, BOOKS AND BOOMS.

'Men, Money and Markets' was the slogan for the 1920s. Just how they expected to build a nation without women I'm not sure but they were sure that they were going to get rich.

Basically, they believed in Progress with a capital P. Australia was seen as the awakening giant. Stanley Melbourne Bruce was the dominant politician of the decade as he thought of the 'Men, Money and Markets' slogan. 'Populate or Perish' was another slogan of the 1920s and 260,927 migrants arrived from Britain to do just that, populate not perish. Closer settlement was seen as the desirable goal. From a population of 5.4 million in 1920, who knows where it could end up; 100 or perhaps 200 million people was seen as possible, probable and desirable. Maximum development rather than optimum or sustainable development was their aim.

HERE TODAY, PAY TOMORROW.

Development occurred all over Australia. The Sydney Harbour Bridge was started in 1923. Western Australia established a dairy industry. South Australia bought trains that were powerful enough to cross the Rockies in North America but were too heavy for the South Australian tracks. Dams were built all over the country; at Eildon in Victoria, Burrinjuck on the Murrumbidgee and the Hume on the Murray itself, which enabled the irrigation of the Riverina to go ahead. The money poured in from London to develop the new industries. The money would, of course, have to be repaid but that would be attended to as the products produced could all be exported and sold on the world market.

Secondary, city-based industries were also to grow for the growing Australian market. A map of Queensland produced at the time boasts about the following growth industries: bedding and upholstery, biscuits, books, ice, jams, soap and pickles. What ever happened to the Queensland pickle industry? Did it get into a jam? Did the jam industry get into a pickle? Queensland also killed over 500,000 koalas in the month of August 1927. Some members of the public were upset, but the government explained the slaughter was intended to support the fur industry. Koala fur is 'not valuable as such' but 'it finds a ready sale for the linings of coats and other outerwear'. (*Australia Through Time* 1997)

Unfortunately, the Roaring Twenties ended dramatically on October 24th 1929. It had been the best of times, now it was going to be the worst of times, the Hungry Thirties.

GREAT, JUST GREAT, ANOTHER GREAT DEPRESSION.

THE FOURTH DECADE. 1930-1939.

How can 30% unemployment and a decade of suffering be called great? The same way that four years of slaughter could be called The Great War. The stories of the suffering and at times heroic response of 'ordinary' Australians is a great story, however, and it is well worth reflecting upon their struggle to survive. To really feel their pain, find a copy of *Weevils in the Flour* by Wendy Lowenstein and read the stories of these battlers. By story I don't mean it is fiction; this story is definitely non-fiction, which means it is not not true.

THE GOOD OLD GOOD OLD DAYS, EVEN IN THE DEPRESSION.

But was it all that bad, really? Surely the good old days were the good old days, not the bad old days? During the period 1928–32 prices fell dramatically. Food prices fell from 1866 to 1425 and housing fell from 1760 to 1374. These are index numbers not dollars or pounds, but the point stands; your money, your pennies, tray-bits, zacks, bobs and quids all 'went further', if you had any, that is. The banana crop went bananas (2.2 to 2.7

million bushels) and apples were apples (5.5 to 9.2) so food was available; no problem there. Melbourne even allowed topless bathing on its beaches in 1938!

Kidding Kids. Kids Not Kidded.

Children stayed longer at school. About 9,000 extra children went to NSW schools in 1932 and attendance improved due to 'the greater attractiveness of school life consequent on improved methods in teaching.' (*Commonwealth Year Book* 1933) Who were they kidding? Not the kids. It was probably because the truant officers were more active or perhaps it was because there were no jobs for the school kids to go to! Get a cloth to wipe up the sarcasm, will you? In the Depression you were also less likely to be the victim of a serious assault as convictions for that offence fell from 431 to 389 from 1929 to 1932. Furthermore, you were far less likely to be annoyed by drunks as convictions for drunkenness fell massively from 57,023 to 37,283. Better education, less crime, less drunkenness, good news all the way.

Perth, Adelaide, Melbourne and Hobart all received above-average rainfall so the weather was okeydoke. Don Bradman, Stan McCabe, Bill Woodfull, Bert Oldfield, Clarrie Grimmett et al cleaned up England again, thrashed them, so things were normal and satisfactory in the sporting arena. At least they were in 1930. We don't talk about 1932. Nor do we mention Phar Lap and April the 5th 1932. 40,667 people must have thought life in Australia was not that bad as in 1932 they migrated to Australia and they all passed the dictation test. They passed it in the sense that they went past, they were all of European descent and didn't have to sit for it. However, 2,132 people, non-Europeans, departed from Australia. 1,165 went or were sent back to China, 287 went or were sent back to Japan and 212 Koepangers went or were sent back to Koepanger, wherever that is. Did they depart voluntarily or were they dictated to depart?

HEALTH BONZER. (O.K.)

People's health also continued to improve. From 1928 to 1932 the number of deaths from measles fell from 201 to 35, whooping cough deaths fell from 237 to 153 and typhoid fever from 168 to 81. I am also pleased to report that only one person died from smallpox and none at all from the plague, which was a lot better than 1921 when 57 died of the plague. The IMR, the infant mortality rate (deaths per 1,000 children under 1) declined from 52.9 to 41.3. Overall, the march of medical science continued throughout the Depression, indeed as it has throughout the whole century. In 1900 the IMR was 103.0 and by 2007 it was down to 4.6, the lowest ever. Again, what was so bad about the 1930s?

WEALTH NOT BONZER. (NOT O.K.)

One-third were out of work! Let me say that again in another way, 1/3rd were out of work! The suffering must have been horrific. Figures, statistics, can get you so far in the study of the human story, but more is required: empathy, an understanding of what it was like to be a person in that situation. One needs to feel what it was like for the child to go to bed hungry and for the mother to wipe her plate with a little gravy so that she could say she had eaten, to save the little available food for her husband and children. One needs to understand, to feel, the humiliation of a man who survived the trenches but couldn't find a job to support his family. They definitely were not the good old days.

WHY WAS IT SO?

However, we need to do more than feel sorry for them. Historians need to understand the events of the past. Why was it so? Let us take a very analytical approach to the rest of this chapter and consider the following questions. How did it start? How did it spread to Australia and why was it so bad in Australia? What action did the government take to overcome the Depression and was this action successful? Who knows, we could learn from history, for once understood, twice avoided.

BACKS TO THE WALL.

Unfortunately, we have been here before (*see* chapter 9 of *The Seriously Weird History of Australia*, Vol 1) so you should be aware of the general causes of economic depressions. It's a mixture of greed and stupidity. People borrow money and invest in get-rich-quick schemes which aren't. In this case the trouble began in New York when Wall Street collapsed; not the street but the Wall Street Stock Exchange; not the building, the price of shares on the Wall Street Stock Exchange. The urgent question on the 24th of October 1929 was not why did it happen but what did it collapse upon? Unfortunately, it collapsed upon the rest of the world. The collapse of the American stock market with a sickening thud led to a sick US economy and when the US economy sneezes the rest of the world catches a cold. Australia was in the category of the 'the rest of the world' and so we caught a cold, a very bad cold, pneumonia.

SPREADING THE WHEEZE WITH THE GREATEST OF EASE.

But how did the American depression become the world Depression? Apparently, when countries don't have any money they don't buy things. Remarkable. Thus America stopped buying things from Australia which meant that we didn't have as much money to buy things from America which meant that America had even less money to buy things from Australia which ... I think you get the picture. And as America stopped buying things from all the other countries such as Britain, Germany and France, Britain, Germany and France stopped buying things such as wool from Australia so we were hit with a double whammy, whatever a whammy is. The triple whammy occurred when America called in its loans from the rest of the world. Less money around to go around, so the merry-go-round of the 1920s stopped.

But how did the Australian wool growers' problem become the problem of the factory worker in Footscray or the new teacher in Mildura? Apparently, the same economic law applies to people as it does to nations; if a farmer, for example, has no money, he spends no money, the shops stop selling and therefore they do not order any new goods from the factory. Bingo. The factory workers who were going to produce the tractor for the farmer or the toaster for the farmer's wife get the sack. At least the teacher is safe as the farmer's children still have to go to school. The government wouldn't sack the teacher, particularly a new government intent on improving the life of ordinary Australians.

'WHAT A FINE MESS YOU HAVE GOT US INTO.' OLIVER HARDY OR STAN LAUREL.

A new Federal Government under James Scullin (ALP) took office on the 22nd of October 1929, two days before the Wall Street collapse. Brilliant timing, just brilliant. The election of 1929 replaced a conservative government that had governed during a decade of prosperity and was defeated largely over issues of industrial relations. The prime minister, Stanley Melbourne Bruce, was even defeated in his own electorate. Thank goodness history does not repeat itself. Move right, along folks, nothing to worry about here.

The Scullin government was faced with the monstrous problem of the Depression. For most people the problem was that they didn't have a job, from the government's point of view the problem was that people with no jobs don't pay taxes, indeed, they actually want some government help, money, for little extras such as food and clothing for their families. The government soon found it was broke, indeed it had a huge deficit. To solve this problem, the government cut back its expenditure and the way it did that was to sack people. Schools just had to make do with fewer teachers. You guessed it; the new teacher at Mildura was dismissed. He had probably survived the bullets of World War I, but in the slang of the times, he 'got the bullet', he was sacked. Great, so the government's response to the unemployment problem was to sack people and increase the numbers unemployed.

HE OTTO BE SACKED.

What happens when a sinking man tries to escape from quicksand? He thrashes around desperately but all the activity only causes the person to sink deeper and deeper into the quicksand. In the Depression the government did the thrashing around but the people did the sinking. Scullin invited Sir Otto Niemeyer, the top banking expert in the world, from the Bank of England no less, to Australia to seek his solution. Sir Otto suggested further sackings. He and most other experts were suffering from a bad case of 'intellectual myopia'. Scullin should have invited another English economist, John Maynard Keynes, to Australia and followed his advice, but that is to jump ahead 20 years in the story.

PAIN BUT NO GAIN.

The Federal Government then met with all the State Premiers to plan a solution. The Premiers Plan of 1931 decided to reduce government expenditure by 20 per cent, to cut wages and interest and to increase taxes. The idea was to ensure that as the national cake was smaller, everyone should receive a smaller slice. The problem was that by taking money out of people's pockets, the government ensured that the national cake just went on shrinking. It fell from £740 million in 1930 to £560 million in 1931. It was a fairly stupid solution. Fair, as it spread the pain roughly equally; stupid, as it only made the Depression worse. No gain without pain, they say, but what is the point of pain but no gain?

DEFAULTS AND VIRTUES OF THE BIG FELLA.

An interesting variation occurred in NSW where the Labor Premier, Jack Lang, faced the same problem as Prime Minister Scullin, but he came up with a different solution. He accepted that he had to cut expenditure to balance his budget, but rather than sack workers he simply defaulted on interest payments on NSW Government debt. Lang just refused to pay the interest on the loans. He argued that it wasn't de fault of the workers that the government had no money, so why should they suffer. Polite society was horrified and said that no-one would ever lend money to NSW again.

The Federal Government paid the bill and passed a law that said Lang had to hand over the money to the Federal Government, but Lang refused to repay the Federal Government. Lang had double-defaulted. The Governor of NSW, Sir Philip Game, said that even the government had to obey the law and Game was game enough to take action and he simply sacked Lang. A new election was called and Lang went to the people with the slogan 'Lang is Right'. But he was too Left for most of the people and he lost the election, and old Lang resigned. He didn't even get to cut the ribbon on the Sydney Harbour Bridge, but that is another story.

BATTLERS BATTLE ON.

Some state and local governments began a sort of work-for-the-dole scheme, the unemployed worked for the 'susso' as it was called. Some built the Great Ocean Road or dug irrigation ditches at Mildura or opened up old gold mines. Many Australians, however, decided that politicians were never going to solve the problem and so they set out to solve their own problems or at least to build their own shelter from the storm. They went rabbiting, fishing, grew their own vegetables and fruit and some went from door to door selling clothes props which they had cut in the bush, or bird baths which they had made from local rock. This was the average man and woman at their noble best.

The swaggie made a re-appearance as men walked the country looking for work. They would often turn up offering to chop wood for a feed. The story is told, well, it is now, of one lady offering a generous slice from a freshly baked cake to a swaggie, only to see the slice left on the plate but the cake snatched and eaten, literally at a gallop.

Lions Led by Lyons.

The Scullin Labor Government was replaced at the election of 1932 by the United Australia Party under Joseph Lyons but the way out of the Depression was to be long and hard. Lyons had also crossed the floor of Parliament, betraying his party, but as he looked so much like a koala, the Labor Party found it difficult to treat him with the same bitterness that they treated Hughes. If Lyons had had as many policies as he had children then the country would have been a good deal better off. He had enough children to field his very own prime minister's eleven. His wife claims that she was the actual person who had the eleven children.

Out of the Frying Pan and into the Fire? No!

To their great credit, however, the people of Australia stuck with democracy, most of them, anyway. In NSW the New Guard was a Fascist organisation and they would have liked the hero of the Great War to take over as a dictator. Monash replied that he had 'no ambition to commit High Treason' and he advised that, 'The only hope for Australia is the ballot-box and an educated electorate.' (Hirst 2002) Monash helps win the war, sets up the electricity grid in Victoria and then stands by democracy when it was under extreme pressure. He's my hero. Are we still allowed to have heroes today, ones that don't kick footballs? As for the Communists, they certainly grew in strength but the appeal of Lang seems to have blunted the appeal of the CPA (Communist Party of Australia) and not many Australian workers went to their Party.

BIG PART OF AUSTRALIA FAILS TO DEPART FROM AUSTRALIA.

The people of Western Australia did decide in a referendum not to stick with Australia. They voted 138,653 to 70,706 to set up their own country as they argued that the protectionist economic policies of Australia were not protecting their economy. They wanted to be free to implement free trade. Fortunately, the British Government decided to overrule their democratic decision and made them stay a part of, rather than part from, Australia. So the Australian continent stayed the Australian Nation and a new New Holland was not to be and we can still call Australia whole.

STORM CLOUDS GATHER DURING STORM.

Unfortunately, not all the rest of the world remained loyal to democracy. Italy was already a Fascist country under Mussolini and Germany under Adolf Hitler followed suit in the 1930s. Britain plodded along with a weak economy but a robust democracy. The USA president did better than the Australian Prime Minister, not at fathering children but at getting his country out of the Depression. Under Franklin Delano Roosevelt and his New Deal, the American economy gradually improved, just in time for another great war.

PS The topless bathing introduced in Melbourne in 1938 was for men only.

WORLD WAR II.

THE FIFTH DECADE. SEPTEMBER 3RD 1939-DECEMBER 16TH 1949.

'It is my melancholy duty to inform you officially that, in consequence of a persistence by Germany in her invasion of Poland, Great Britain has declared war upon her, and that, as a result, Australia is also at war.' So said Robert Gordon Menzies on September 3rd 1939 when he informed Australians that again we were at war. There were a few people in Australia who wanted Australia to take the position of Switzerland or Eire and stay neutral, but not many. This time, however, there would be no wild enthusiasm; no 'Home-by-Christmas' naïve optimism, just quiet resolve to do what had to be done.

RATS, HERE WE GO AGAIN.

From the Australian point of view the first two years of World War WII were similar to World War I. The second Australian Imperial Force (AIF) sailed to Egypt and performed heroic and noble deeds, particularly the rats of Tobruk. But in fact the war was quite different. Firstly, it was a war of movement with tanks and dive bombers and secondly, the Allies, our side, wasn't winning. By mid-1940, the Germans had defeated France, Russia was still not in the war and many in the USA were still pretending not to notice that democracy was under threat.

'THEIR FINEST HOUR'.

Basically it was only Britain and its empire that held out against a Nazi victory and even then it was touch and go. The British just managed to save their army at Dunkirk when hundreds of small boats helped rescue the troops on the beaches and return them to Britain. The Luftwaffe, the German air force, then attacked Britain to soften it for invasion but suffered its first defeat at the hands of the Royal Air Force (RAF). At the end of the battle, the British Prime Minister, Winston Churchill, made his famous speech, telling the British people and the world, that 'Never in the field of human conflict was so much owed by so many to so few.' Ten Australians were among the 'few' who died serving in the RAF in the Battle of Britain.

GOING, GOING...

But then suddenly the war came home to Australia when the Japanese attacked the US fleet at Pearl Harbor on 7th December 1941. Three days later, the Japanese sank the *Repulse* and *The Prince of Wales,* Britain's two capital ships. On the 23rd they took Wake Island and on the 26th Hong Kong fell. The Americans were driven out of the Philippines, the Dutch out of Indonesia, the French out of Indo-China and the British out of

Malaya and Burma and were now on the defensive in India itself. And then came the great shock. On 15th February Singapore was surrendered to the Japanese and 15,384 Australian troops became prisoners of war. Four days later, Darwin was attacked. As Henry Lawson predicted, 'The foreign foe was at our harbour-gate', and Australia was isolated and virtually defenseless.

Not quite Curtains but Curtin.

Fortunately, the man in charge was John Curtin. He was hard-working, intelligent and courageous. His most important contribution was to face the reality that Britain could no longer defend Australia: 'We know that Australia can go and Britain can still hold on. We are determined that Australia shall not go.' Australia, he said, in December 1941, had to 'look to America'. (*The Herald* 27th December 1941) This, by the way, was six weeks before the fall of Singapore.

Unfortunately, he never lived to see the successful outcome of WWII as he died in office, basically from hard work. He was so honest that he bought postage stamps and if he made a personal phone call while at Parliament House, say, to tell his wife he would be home late for dinner, he would tear up a stamp as payment. He was not only honest, he also had a touch of shyness and modesty. He would often slip into a sportsground to watch a quarter of football or an hour or two of cricket. Anonymously, without any press coverage!

Curtin did capture the national mood perfectly. In this crisis the nation found a determination and a resolve to hang on to what we had that must have surprised themselves as well as our enemies. Dame Mary

Gilmore, a poet of the Left, expressed this complex, confused, steely determination when she wrote in her disturbing poem, 'Nationality':

'I have grown past hate and bitterness
I see the world as one,
Yet though I can no longer hate,
My son is still my son.

All men at God's round table sit.
And all men must be fed.
But this loaf in my hand,
This loaf is my son's bread!'

'I'LL BE BACK'. FIRST DRAFT OF MACARTHUR'S SPEECH.

The American General, Douglas MacArthur, fled the Philippines pledging 'I shall return.' Initially, he set up headquarters in St Kilda Road, Melbourne, to begin the counter attack, but this was seen as just a little bit too far from the action and he moved his headquarters to Brisbane. Soon, huge numbers of US troops arrived in Australia to prepare the counter-attack. This of course created some tensions in Australia as the Yanks were said to be over paid, over sexed and over here. In one famous incident near Brisbane an Australian troop train was stopped alongside an American troop train. They tried to avoid that situation from then on. 'Thanks but no yanks' was the view of some people but the huge majority of people were grateful for American chewing gum, stockings, dollars and the overwhelming power they delivered against the enemy.

You're Checked, 'Mate'.

The Japanese soon found out that the attack on Pearl Harbor had not totally eliminated the US Pacific Fleet. An invasion force heading towards Port Moresby, New Guinea, was defeated at the Battle of the Coral Sea and the Battle of Midway even more decisively turned the tide in the Pacific. On land, the Japanese were also checked on the Kokoda Track by Australian troops as the Japanese tried to attack Port Moresby over the Owen Stanley Ranges. The Battle of Milne Bay was even more decisive.

At Milne Bay, 2,800 Japanese marines were put ashore to attack Port Moresby by working their way along the south coast of New Guinea. They were defeated and only 1,318 were evacuated. Under Major General Cyril Clowes, Australian troops, some of them veterans of Tobruk, had broken the spell of Japanese invincibility. This was the first time the Japanese were not merely delayed, they were beaten. The Japanese had made the same mistake as we had made at Gallipoli: they had landed their troops in the wrong spot, 11 miles out in their case, and they made the same mistake as the British made with the *Repulse* and *The Prince of Wales*. They did not have control of the air, the Royal Australian Air Force (RAAF) did. The rest of the war in the Pacific would be a long and bloody retreat for the Japanese. It was just as long and bloody for the Australians and the Americans but for the Australians and the Americans it was not a retreat.

THE HOME FRONT BURNING.

This time, however, the war did come home to Australia. Darwin was attacked and 250 died, of whom 188 were American sailors aboard the destroyer USS Peary. Nine other Australian towns including Broome, Derby and Townsville were also attacked. Twenty-nine merchant ships were sunk by Japanese submarines off the coast of Australia during the war. Schools had working bees to dig trenches in case of air attack and the whole of Australia was placed on a brownout. A blackout was briefly tried but driving around at night with no headlights at all caused more trouble than it solved. One factory was uncertain what the difference was between a brownout and a blackout so they blacked out every second window. This produced a massive draught board that could be seen on the clouds for miles. Weirdly ineffective.

The dramatic events of May 31st 1942 when three Japanese two-man midget submarines, armed with two torpedoes each, entered Sydney Harbour, really brought the war home to Sydneysiders. The enemy was not just at our harbour gate, they had penetrated it. Like the attack on Darwin, their target was a US ship, the USS Chicago which a spy plane, launched from an off-shore submarine, had spotted the night before. The one submarine that fired at the USS Chicago missed but struck the converted ferry HMAS Kuttabul, killing 21 sailors. There must have been great confusion on the harbour that night as the night ferries continued to run throughout the engagement. Well, people still had to get home from the pictures, you know. At about the same time, a spy plane, launched from a submarine just outside the Heads at Port Phillip Bay, flew over the industrial suburbs of Melbourne, so Melbourne was lucky not to suffer the same fate.

WOMEN, WORK AND THE WAR.

This time there was no conscription debate to split the unity of the nation. Women in particular played a very active role with nearly 70,000 enlisting in the services. Their heroic deeds were numerous as they shared the dangers and fortunes of the men. The sinking of the hospital ship *Centaur* in May 1943 just off the Queensland coast is just one example. Although the ship was clearly marked as a hospital ship, it was still sunk by a Japanese submarine in broad daylight. Of the 363 people on board, only 64 survived. Of the 12 nurses, only one, Sister Savage, was rescued from the shark-infested waters.

> 'For men must work, and women must weep
> And the sooner it's over, the sooner we sleep.'

It was not just men who worked, however, women were also involved in direct war work, 184,000 of them by 1943. They worked as cooks, hairdressers, typists and waitresses. They also worked as electricians, motor mechanics, aircraft refuellers, welders and butchers. They even dressed differently with the services issuing women with slacks. But they were not slack, they were young, earnest, loyal, and full of fun and they performed a huge amount of vital work. They certainly wept as 30,000 Australians died but they also worked and in so doing they helped win the war and to change themselves and their country in the process.

MEANWHILE, BACK IN EUROPE...

Fortunately, the megalomaniac Adolf Hitler, thwarted in his attempt to attack Britain, attacked the USSR (Russia). Communist Russia and Democratic Britain were now allies. It wasn't fortunate for the Russians but, like Napoleon before him, Hitler learnt about the immense size of Russia and the severity of its winters. In another stroke of stupidity, Hitler also declared war on the USA after the Japanese attack on Pearl Harbor. After D Day 1944, Germany was slowly squeezed from both sides until 8th May 1945 when Hitler's Third Reich came to an end.

Democracy had triumphed. Britain had provided the time, Russia the blood and the USA the money. Democracy didn't triumph in Russia or Eastern Europe, of course, where the war saw the survival of another tyranny, an extended and powerful tyranny. But one can only deal with one tyranny at a time and Europe was grateful for peace. Europe also had to face the full extent of the crimes of national socialism, fascism, when the concentration camps were discovered. How could they have killed children?

'BATTLERS AND BALTS' FROM AROUND THE WORLD.

The Polish people who suffered so much were bitterly disappointed that one can only deal with one tyranny at a time. So were millions of other Eastern Europeans, people from the Baltic countries, the Ukraine, Yugoslavia. who were either trapped behind the 'iron curtain' or who fled west to the West and became 'Displaced Persons'. One 16-year-old girl who lived and worked in Gdansk nursed the soldiers of both the Russian and German armies as they rolled through her native Poland. Her strongest memory was of unwinding the bandages to see how many toes and fingers were left after frostbite had done its work. Why did she choose to come to Australia? She chose Australia as it was as far away as she could get from the war zone that was Europe. Good choice.

A young Yugoslav who survived the war working as a POW on German farms selected Australia over the USA or Canada as he did not want to be anywhere near Al Capone et al. He wanted to go to a land that had sunshine, food, free education, peace and freedom. Out he came on the purpose built *SS Skaugum* and after a time at Bonegilla army camp near Albury he began his new life at the International Harvester Company, Geelong. I hope he wrote a diary. What a fascinating story he has to tell.

What were their impressions of this huge empty land with weird trees and even weirder animals? Can he remember his first ice-cream? It was probably a Dixie.

WAR AND PEACE IN THE PACIFIC.

The Pacific War, now there is a nice contradiction in terms, finally ended in 1945 after the Americans had dropped two atomic bombs on Japan and threatened them with a third which they didn't have at the time. Australian troops were used in mopping-up operations in the Pacific in places such as Timor and Wewak in New Guinea. On the 2nd of September 1945 the Japanese signed the surrender on the US battleship *Missouri* in Tokyo Bay and the Australian general, Sir Thomas Blamey, signed for Australia. The Australian public followed the dancing man through the streets to celebrate peace. Then the POWs came home from notorious camps such as Changi and Australia had to weep again as they found out the full extent of the horror these men had endured. 8031 never returned, whereas only 129 Australian POWs died in WWI.

Unlike WWI, when Australia played a key role in the defeat of Germany, WWII saw Australia concentrate her efforts in our own part of the world. This has made for an interesting and at times bitter division in the way people interpret the role of Australia in WWII. For some, like Paul Keating, the war is largely seen as a war of national survival against a Japanese attempt to capture this land. They emphasise 'The Battle for Australia'. Others take a more international view of the war and argue that there was no battle for Australia and that essentially WWII was a struggle between democracy and fascism and Australia played only 'a small part of the great Allied coalition, in which the most significant battles occurred far away'. (Dr Stanley, Australian War Memorial Anniversary Oration, 2006)

AFTER THE WAR WAS OVER.

Winston Churchill was shocked to lose the British election in 1945 to the British Labour Party led by Clement Attlee. The British people were grateful for Churchill's leadership during the war, but in 1945 they wanted a better world, not a return to the unemployment of the 1930s. In Australia the Party of Curtin was not thrown out at the election as the Australian Labor Party had not only provided united leadership during the war, it also had a plan for the peace. How could freedom and prosperity be achieved? 'Socialism' was the answer according to the ALP and the electorate agreed with them.

The new Prime Minister, Ben Chifley, took his pipe out of his mouth and got on with it. Unemployment benefits were introduced, scholarships to university for ex-servicemen and now 'uniform taxation' – so the Federal Government had exclusive power to levy income tax and therefore had the money to implement its program.

The Snowy Mountains scheme was also inaugurated. It was designed to divert water that was taking a short-cut to the sea via the Snowy River, over the Snowy Mountains so it would take the long cut to the sea via the Murray River. On the way it could generate electricity and grow oranges. Irrigation and industrial development in the one development.This scheme also highlighted the new extended migration program introduced by the ALP under Arthur Calwell. Now, all Europeans were encouraged to come and develop Australia. This was not only an economic policy, it was a policy of defence. 'Populate or perish' was the lesson that many Australians took out of WWII. Strangely, it was also the lesson they took out of WWI.

However, in 1949 the electorate changed its mind about how prosperity and freedom could be achieved. Robert Gordon Menzies was back. 'Freedom and prosperity can be achieved not by socialism but by free enterprise,' said Menzies and the electorate agreed with him that the ALP policy of nationalising the banks was too Left bank, I mean Left wing for them. They didn't agree with Menzies when he said we needed to ban the Communist Party to secure our freedom. Too Right wing.

Wars are usually followed by peace and peace usually brings prosperity.This generation had survived the Depression and they had defeated a threat to democracy and their nation's freedom. They deserved more than a few Happy Days. They deserved a happy decade, or two or three.

Is Heaven Boring?

The Sixth Decade. 1950-59.

On no account must you admit that you admire the 1950s as the 50s are seen as the worst possible time, worse than the hungry thirties or the warring forties. The fifties are seen as boring. They are also condemned for being single cultural (it's the opposite of multi cultural), racist, sexist, and apparently only one type of cheese was obtainable.

However, it is conceded that people were happy, enjoyed themselves, drove to the beach and ate ice-creams, felt safe and had a strong sense of family and neighbourhood. It is said that people didn't even bother to lock their doors or build front fences, whereas walking down the same street today all one hears is the barking of the huge guard dogs behind the two-metre fences. But that is seen as being of little importance. It was boring and it was boring because they didn't bring in enough changes! Is any of this true? Were the 1950s the happy days or the boring days? Was it a period of stalemate with no significant changes being introduced?

It is very difficult to actually prove that people are happy or bored but the generation who grew up in the fifties is still around in their millions; they are the baby boomers so you can ask them yourself. The baby boomers were babies and children during this decade and the Happy Little Vegemite advertisement certainly suggests that they had a happy childhood. But 'Collins St at 5 o'clock', a great painting by John Brack in the National Gallery of Victoria suggests their parents were not so happy as they were stuck in the rat race, working nine to five just to make a living.

BUTCHERS, BAKERS BUT NO CANDLESTICK MAKERS.

But as for the accusation that the decade saw no significant change, that is nonsense. At the start of the fifties the housewife stayed at home and raised 3.5 kids. How did she do the shopping if she was at home all the time? Everything was delivered. Eight 'tradesmen' visited the typical house each week. The butcher, the baker, no, not the candlestick maker but the grocer, the milkie, the insurance man, the Rawleigh's man, the Minister and even the ice man cometh. The best part was that they came around with a horse and cart and you haven't seen anything until you have seen a milk cart charging headlong up the street being pulled by a bolting horse.

However, by the end of the 1950s all this was going, as the new Supermarkets came in. This, combined with more efficient means of housework and smaller families, meant that a woman could now be a mother and a wife without being a housewife. By 1960, many a wife chose to stay in or re-join the workforce and become a workwife. No, that's not the word, a working mother. Men as yet were not called working fathers or househusbands.

Before they were married, the influence of American films and American television shows meant that the girls were sometimes called 'Baby' or 'Baby Doll' by their boyfriends. How can such terms be used about an adult without giving offense? They definitely could not have been used about a man without a punch-up occurring. The 1950s were a little bit weird.

A Man's Home is His Triple-Fronted Cream Brick Veneer.

The 1950s saw the sprawl of the suburbs as everyone who could moved out of the crowded inner-city suburbs and out to an outer-city suburb and into their own triple-fronted cream brick veneer house on a quarter-acre block with rotary clothes line and motor mower. At first it was fairly difficult to build a triple-fronted cream brick veneer as there was a shortage of materials. People became tired of waiting for a builder and began the do-it-yourself craze. They even experimented with flat roofs to save timber because, with everything in short supply, prices began to soar. Inflation had been invented. Actually, it was reinvented as the older people remembered it from World War I.

HAH! They call THIS inflation!? Remember 1917? Now THAT was some REAL inflation!

APPALLING, SPRAWLING SUBURBS REPLACE APPALLING, OVERCROWDED SLUMS.

They soon found out that the solution to one problem creates its own set of problems. The outer suburbs, usually described as the 'sprawling' suburbs, were inadequately connected with all the services that a family requires. Sometimes the service required was something basic such as sewerage or sealed roads but the government was also faced with the urgent need for public buildings such as kindergartens and schools as virtually nothing had been built for twenty years. I hope you are not sitting in one as you read this chapter. They are ugly. The problem was made worse by the lack of public transport. Usually, it was a one-car family and the father drove it to his work in the city, or on the other side of town, leaving the mother at home isolated with poor public transport to get to the Doctor or the new Supermarket.

GOOD, GOOD, GOOD, MIGRATION.

The change that really surprised everyone was that, instead of returning to the old pre-war days of high unemployment, there was actually a shortage of workers. What was even more surprising was that unemployment stayed low for the whole decade yet at the same time migrants poured into the country. About 1.5 million migrants arrived between 1945 and 1959. It is interesting to graph unemployment and migration on the one graph. Right throughout the 1950s there was very high migration but unemployment never went beyond 2 per cent. In the 1930s there was very low migration but very high unemployment.

So, contrary to expectations, does high migration cause full employment? Does low migration cause unemployment? Just because A occurs before or with B doesn't prove that A causes B, you know. The Aztecs always sacrificed a prisoner to the gods each morning to make sure the sun came up. They thought A caused B. It didn't.

The pool of potential migrants from Britain was soon exhausted and the government widened the program to include Dutch, Germans, Italians and Greeks. These New Australians were encouraged to assimilate into mainstream Australia. They were referred to as New Australians rather than as Ukrainian-Australians or Polish-Australians. This migration policy has been judged a brilliant success although of course it was not without its problems as non English speaking children soon found out in the classroom. The schoolyard also had its difficulties. One little Italian boy had a special fence picket on his way to school in Carlton. On one side he spoke Italian and on the other side he spoke English.

'Your Shout, Mate.'

A further difficulty occurred as the language spoken in Australian schoolyards, shops and factories, was not quite the English the migrants were formally taught in school. John O'Grady explores the confusion around the Aussie use of the word 'shout' to marvelous effect in his book *They're a Weird Mob*. To get served in a pub in the 6 o'clock crush for last drinks, one had to shout, so to an Aussie to shout was to buy a drink for a mate. To the New Australian, to shout at your friend was simple rudeness. November the 5th, Cracker Night, when all the talk would have been about penny bungers, Catherine wheels, jumping jacks and fizzers, must have been particularly confusing.

WE NEVER HAD IT SO GOOD WITH SO MANY GOODS.

Economic changes continued throughout the 1950s as factories were converted to peacetime production. In 1957, Menzies signed the Australia-Japan Trade agreement and by 1966 Japan had become the largest importer of Australian goods. In the past century, Australia prospered as we provided raw materials for the British Industrial Revolution and in return we received British manufactured goods. After WWII we would no longer be a mere farm and mine for Britain. Now, we would be a farm and a mine for Japan. Our prosperity continued with real national production increasing by 66 per cent between 1948 and 1961. We were becoming a consumer society, each household with its own refrigerator and even Australia's own car, the Holden, which was 100 per cent American-owned. For most Australians the problem was not how to produce wealth but how to consume it.

CULTURAL CONS AND CULTURAL ICONS.

The intellectuals were of course, as usual, appalled at the shallowness of the rest of the human race. This wealth, they said, is destroying our national soul. Anyway, it could not last, argued Donald Horne in *The Lucky Country*. Most Australians missed the irony and took the lucky country as a fair and accurate description of our country and simply settled down to enjoy our luck. Edna Everage (Barry Humphries the satirist) worried about what was called 'the cultural cringe' as Australian artists felt they had to go overseas to prove to the world that they were of world standard. It was true that overseas visitors were asked their opinion of Australia virtually before they were off the plane, which does suggest that we lacked confidence in our own judgment.

Popular culture certainly changed in the 1950s. The movies still had Chips Rafferty, and Slim Dusty's 'The Pub with No Beer' was the hit song of 1957. We still sang 'Waltzing Matilda' at the Melbourne Olympics and we still had our own sporting heroes including Betty Cuthbert, Russell Mockridge, Richie Benaud, Dawn Fraser and Lew Hoad. However, a new creature was invented called the teenager; they had money, jobs, a motorbike and their own attitudes. They even had their own sort of antisocial behaviour. It was called juvenile delinquency. They listened to Bill Haley and the Comets and to some American singer called Mr E Presley. To the older generation, the Coca-Colonisation of Australia, particularly young Australia, was deplorable. But it was only the beginning, as television was introduced in 1956.

Labor Strikes Out.

Politically, there were also big changes. The Labor Party which had ruled Australia for ten years lost power in 1949 and then for the third time it split. Three strikes and you are out and the Labor Party was out and the Liberal Party, led by its founder Sir Robert Gordon Menzies, was to stay in power for the next 23 years. Menzies was a brilliant speaker who based his success on 'the forgotten people', the middle class. He called them the forgotten people because he didn't like the idea of mentioning social class in a classless society although of course Australia wasn't. Under socialism, he said, society was like a stagnant pond and in stagnant ponds the scum rises to the surface. Nice.

Does it make any difference which party is in power? It's hard to tell as it is not possible to re-run history like an experiment in science, but Menzies certainly continued with many of the policies of the Labor Party. He continued with high immigration, social welfare and the expansion of secondary and university education, so perhaps the differences would not have been that great. The Menzies Building at Monash University may have been called Evatt Hall after the Labor leader.

Menzies' success was largely the result of the long economic boom and the resulting very low unemployment levels of the 1950s. Should Menzies get the credit? No, it was coincidence, a fluke, said his Labor opponents. But Menzies had learnt from the economist John Maynard Keynes that governments can smooth out, but not eradicate, the roller-coaster ride of free market capitalism. If things are slowing down, step on the accelerator with more government spending; that will increase employment. If things are going too fast, then touch the brake with cuts to government spending; that will reduce inflation. But what if unemployment and inflation happen at the same time? Well, then, you put one foot on the accelerator and the other foot on the brake. Look, don't worry about it. That didn't, can't, won't happen. Didn't in the 1950s, anyway.

Menzies even continued to support the policy of seeking US protection in our foreign policy, which is a little surprising for a man who was British to the bootstraps. He 'did but see her passing by' in 1954 when, as Prime Minister, he welcomed the young Queen Elizabeth II to Australia. But he also ensured that Australia had an insurance policy called ANZUS which stated that, if attacked, Australia and New Zealand would charge in to help save the USA. Menzies was actually interested in the reverse clause but like all insurance policies it wasn't actually watertight. The parties only agreed to consult each other if difficulties should arise.

Hot and Cold Running Wars.

Unfortunately, the world of the 1950s was not a peaceful one. The Allies from World War II became bitter enemies and the world divided between the Communist world of the USSR and Red China and the 'Free' or 'Capitalist' world depending on your bias, led by the USA. Australia became involved in this conflict in places such as Berlin, Korea and Malaya. Menzies was able to use the red-yellow peril to convince many Australians that we were threatened internally as well as externally. He tried, but failed, to ban the Communist Party of Australia, which at the time definitely could not fit into a phone box. However, it had quite a deal of influence. The conflict ran hot and cold for the next 50 years but fortunately it was not resolved by the weapons of the super powers. MAD as it was, mutually assured destruction worked. The super powers did not go to war, at least not against each other.

CIRCULAR PROGRESS.

Some people, including Henry Ford, believe that History just doesn't make any sense. It's just one damned thing after another. Optimists believe that History is a positive story of human progress. Pessimists believe that there is a pattern, but the pattern they see is the negative one of civilisations being born, flowering and then declining. In Australian History, there does seem to be a pattern of good times, bad times and then a war followed by good times etc. And at first glance the 1950s looks like a recycled 1920s without the unemployment. I have a compromise to suggest between the optimists and the pessimists. History is a circle but, like a wheel when it completes a revolution, it also moves forward. What do you think of this theory? It isn't patented so you can use it.

In the 1950s this would all have been dismissed as nonsense. The baby boomers and their parents believed in Progress and the evidence was in front of their eyes. The human story was the story of humankind's journey from caves to triple-fronted cream brick veneers.

TURBULENT, TUMULTUOUS, TEENAGERS.

THE SEVENTH 'DECADE.' 1960-2ND DECEMBER 1972.

From this point on, the chapters will get smaller and smaller. Why? Are recent times less important or less complex? Certainly not. Is it harder to write recent history? Certainly is. The problem is that, to get a clear picture of the causes and consequences of any event, the dust needs to settle. Today, for example, we are still looking through the dust that was raised by the attack on the Twin Towers on 9/11 and we are still looking through the dust caused by the drying-up of our rivers and our land.

Furthermore, the ongoing debate on 'current history', if that is not a contradiction in terms, often produces more heat than light as most of us were victims, benefactors, participants or biased spectators in these events. Historians should tread carefully into the discussion of recent events and leave it up to politicians to race confidently and assertively forward with all 'the answers'. At least in Opposition, politicians confidently race forward with all the answers. They do find a few problems in their answers once in power. Historians need only hindsight to answer their questions; politicians require a much more elusive attribute: foresight.

RADICAL APPROACH TO THE SWINGING SIXTIES.

It is said that to understand the present we need to study the past. You sure? That makes about as much sense as saying that, to understand the geography of Australia, open your atlas at the map of India! Surely if you want to understand the present you should study the present? Never trust an unexamined cliché. Does an understanding of the 1960s require an understanding of the 1950s? In any case, sometimes the next decade is not a continuation of the trends of the previous decade but a deliberate swing away from the previous decade; and that's the contention of this chapter about the swinging sixties. The 1960s were a swing away from the certainties of the fifties, so to study the sixties we will examine the sixties. Radical. And it was.

The generation that 'fought' the Depression and WWII and secured our freedom was shocked that when they gave this freedom to their children, the now grown up baby boomers actually used it. The baby boomer generation inherited not only a free society, they had wealth and education and the contraceptive pill and, increasingly, their own car. These factors gave them unprecedented personal freedom to make their own decisions about life. But why were they radical? Why did they want to change the world? What was so wrong with the free and prosperous world that had been handed to them at such great cost by their parents? The first hint that young people got that the free world wasn't perfect was when some of them lost their freedom. They were conscripted into the army for two years' service and some of them were sent to war.

GIVE WAR A CHANCE.

It was a war that sort of sneaked up on us. Menzies had to tell us on June 30th 1965, 'We are at war. Make no mistake about it.' Many thought the war a mistake, full stop. The conscripts who went to Vietnam certainly knew that they were at war. It was the young, as always, who would pay the price for the war, but not all the young. Menzies announced the original commitment, but he retired in January 1966 and it was Harold Holt who increased the task force to include conscripts. If your birth date was selected in a lottery then your lot was two years' conscription in the defence forces and a possible spell in Vietnam. If your birth date wasn't selected, your lot was to join the lot enjoying themselves in the swinging sixties. Your lot depended a lot on the lottery.

In Vietnam, the regulars and the conscripts fought a difficult guerrilla war against the Vietcong. Australia lost over 500 men, including 202 conscripts, in the conflict. The Battle of Long Tan cost Australia 18 dead and the Battle of Coral/Balmoral was nearly as deadly. It was said that to win we needed to win the hearts and minds of the Vietnamese. In the end it was the failure to win the hearts and minds of the Australian and American public that led to the withdrawal from Vietnam and the eventual takeover of the whole of Vietnam by the Communists.

GIVE PEACE A CHANCE.

The war, and in particular the use of conscripts, produced a huge anti-war movement. Led by politicians including Jim Cairns and Tom Uren, the 'foot soldiers' of the peace movement, if that is an appropriate term, were young university students. Huge anti-war rallies were held, the largest in Melbourne in May 1970 when 70,000 took part in the Vietnam Moratorium. Strange word; it means a suspension or cessation, but at the time many thought it had something to do with mortuaries. The protestors, the 'peaceniks' as they were called by their opponents, chanted bitter slogans such as 'LBJ, LBJ, How many kids did you kill today?' but the main chant was 'Get off my foot. Get off my foot.' It was a very big, squashy march.

Some protestors did more than peacefully protest, they threw paint at the American President's car when he toured Melbourne. President Lyndon Baines Johnson, the LBJ referred to in the previous paragraph, wasn't hit, but his young, red-blooded, all-American bodyguard, young Rufus Youngblood, lived up to his name as he was covered in red paint. Some protestors went further still; they not only opposed the law, they refused to obey it. They became draft dodgers.

TIMED OUT.

In 1966, the Labor Party, which was opposed to the war, was trounced at the federal election when they won only 41 seats out of 124. The war was popular, or acceptable anyway, to the electorate. In 1969, however, Labor increased its number to 59. The Liberal leader, Sir William McMahon, saw the writing on the wall and withdrew the troops. When the ALP under Gough Whitlam won the next election on December 2nd 1972, with 67 seats, he ended conscription and released draft resisters from jail on December the 5th, his third day in office. 'It's Time,' he said and the Australian public agreed with him that it was time, time to get out.

It was never clear whether the troops were withdrawn because we had won or because we had lost or because it wasn't worth the cost of winning or because we didn't want to win, but anyway the troops were brought home and Vietnam was left to its fate. The Welcome Home Parade was held on Oct 3rd 1987, 15 years after they came home. The Vietnam Memorial was placed in Anzac Parade, Canberra, in 1993, 20 years after they came home. No wonder the Vietnam vets felt unappreciated.

'THE YOUNG ARE REVOLTING'.

However, by now the young were not merely questioning the policies and wisdom of their elders on the war, they were raising other questions about life in Australia and indeed about life in general. Charles Perkins led a freedom ride through NSW and demanded equal treatment for Aboriginal people, even in the local swimming pools. Taking their cue from Woodstock, a flower power movement developed in Australia. The Nimbin festival shocked older Australians as hippies simply dropped out of what they considered was a rat race. With their long hair and weird clothing, it looked to the older generation as though they had dropped out of the human race.

THE END OF INNOCENCE, AGAIN.

Crime exists in every decade, of course, but at times a crime is committed that reaches a new low and makes us despair of humanity. We are horrified when the first Australian case occurs as we associate some crimes, drugs, kidnapping, or terrorism, for example, with other countries and cultures. Unfortunately, the evidence proves otherwise. The 1960s had its fair share of crimes and it began with a terrible shock to Australian innocence when Graeme Thorne, the child of an Opera House lottery winner, was kidnapped and murdered. In 1966, the Beaumont children disappeared from a beach in Adelaide.

AUSTRALIA'S LAST LEGAL EXECUTION.

The deaths of George Hobson and Arthur Henderson were another low point of the sixties. Hobson was the prison warder at Pentridge shot when two prisoners escaped. Henderson was a tow-truck driver who was shot dead by one of the escapees when he recognised them. This is the Ronald Ryan, Peter Walker, escape. They were caught after two weeks on the run and Ryan was sentenced to death for the murder of Hobson. A huge anti-hanging campaign fought for a reprieve but Ryan was not reprieved. Walker served 19 years in jail and still says that Ryan was innocent of the murder of George Hobson, but he himself was guilty of Henderson's murder. Walker also says he is still haunted nightly by the faces of Ryan, Hobson and Henderson.

r_pri_v_

A HALT TO HOLT CONSPIRACIES.

A short but potentially dangerous comment is required on the death of Harold Holt. Never print conspiracy theories as once printed, twice believed, they are off and running like a bushfire. You just cannot get conspiracy theories out of some people's heads. Hitler is still alive in South America according to some people, even though he was born in 1889. On December 22nd 1967, the Prime Minister, Harold Holt, drowned at Portsea, Victoria. I repeat the fact. Harold Holt drowned on December 22nd 1967. I do wish, however, that they had not named a swimming pool in his memory.

Sporting Ties and Hatless Tasks.

We were still a sport-obsessed nation. In 1961, the West Indies and Australia played the first ever tied Test. In the process they revitalised Test cricket and in so doing the West Indians played a role in breaking down racism. The Melbourne Cup of 1965 was famous, not for the fact that Light Fingers won, but for the fact that the English model, Jean Shrimpton, turned up without a hat and in a short dress. She was actually appropriately dressed for Australian summer conditions. Scandalous! How dare she!

So the swinging sixties was a time when the idealistic young baby boomers questioned the policies, purpose and beliefs of an older generation of Australians. It is easy enough to ask questions; the question is, did the baby boomers have any answers when it was their turn to make the decisions? We shall see.

AT OUR WHITLAM'S END.

THE EIGHTH 'DECADE'. 1972-82.

In 1972, the 'Men and women of Australia' agreed that, 'It's time,' but time for what? For reform, for renewal, for a reconstructed Australia, and Edward Gough Whitlam and his deputy Lance Barnard wasted no time in getting started with a program of social, political and cultural reforms after the ALP won the December 1972 election. For 14 days just the two of them ran the country, Whitlam had 13 Ministries and Barnard had the other 14. It's called a duumvirate. The country, however, soon ran into economic trouble and the general rule is that economic trouble for the country usually ends up as financial and political trouble for the government. It is said that the exception proves the rule but in this case the rule proved the rule. The Whitlam Government was soon in political trouble.

THE MCI. (MINIMUM CHIPS INDEX)

In 1970, inflation stood at 5 per cent. By 1973, it was running at 10 per cent. It was galloping at 17.5 per cent after the oil price rises of the next year; we had a bad case of galloping inflation. Retirees were distressed, distraught and devastated; wage earners were surprised, stunned and shocked, and my pocket money was seriously depleted. A minimum serve of chips at the local chippies, Steve's, was 5c prior to the oil crisis. Today, at the same shop, it is $2.50. At this rate it will be over $100 for 'minimum chips' by the middle of this century. This was and is serious. The

MCI, the minimum chips index, is not actually an official measure of inflation, but it makes more sense to most Australians than the Treasury Underlying Consumer Price Index.

INFLATED UNEMPLOYMENT FIGURES.

Worse was to come as the unions were shaken and stirred into action. They demanded wage rises to compensate for the price rises and so the wage-price spiral, which was to last for 15 years, began. Soon these wage rises led to cut-backs in employment and the unemployment rate also began to rise. It doubled from 2.5 per cent in 1972 to 5 per cent in 1976. Now we had inflation and unemployment at the same time. The economy was moving along too quickly and too slowly, so clearly the economy needed to be speeded up and slowed down at the same time, simultaneously, concurrently. Tricky. How do you deal with a flood and a fire when they occur concurrently? Which one do you deal with first? The 1970s gave the same answers as they would have given in the 1950s. We don't know, we really don't know.

The leader of Her Majesty's Loyal Opposition, Malcolm Fraser (Liberal), decided that the first thing that had to be dealt with was the removal of the government. The leader of Her Majesty's Government, Gough Whitlam (ALP), decided that that was not required. Right, said Fraser, then we will block the budget in the Senate and you will have no money to run the country and you will have to resign. Imagine all those public servants not getting paid, nothing would get done. This is not a time for cheap shots at public servants. In the words of Stan Cross' great cartoon, 'For gorsake, stop laughen: this is serious'. (*Smith's Weekly* 29th July 1933) No pensions would have been paid, for a start.

CHOOSE YOUR OWN PARAGRAPH.

One could tell the story of the dismissal of the Whitlam Government in a balanced, careful way, ensuring that the argument is fairly stated. One could, but that would make this dramatic event uneventful. I will write two paragraphs, blatantly biased, one from Fraser's viewpoint and the other from Whitlam's viewpoint. Then it is up to you as to which paragraph you will read and retain and which one you will read and delete.

Pick a Box

The government had, said Fraser, 'created inflation and unemployment not experienced for 40 years' and therefore it did not deserve to govern. (Hirst 2002) The Senate, in which we, the Liberals, have the numbers, will not pass the Budget until Whitlam calls an election. The power of the Senate to withhold supply, money, was written into the constitution and therefore we are acting constitutionally in blocking supply. 'The continuing incompetence, deceit, and duplicity' of the Prime Minister means that if Whitlam will not call an election then he deserves to be dismissed. So said Malcolm Fraser.

My government has a mandate (and presumably a womandate) to govern this country and to implement our reforms, said Whitlam. The ALP has a majority in the House of Representatives, the People's House and therefore 'has a right to expect that it will be able to govern'. The Senate is only a House of Review and the threats of the Senate are a 'grave threat to the principles of responsible government and parliamentary government in Australia'. (Hirst 2002) Fraser's case for dismissal is dismissed as an attack not only on the democratically elected government, but also on Democracy itself. So said Gough Whitlam.

DEFIANT WHITLAM DEFEATED.

Whitlam held his nerve but not the reins of government as the Governor General, Sir John Kerr, decided that he had to act to break the deadlock and he dismissed Whitlam, appointed Fraser as caretaker Prime Minister and called an election. Whitlam called Fraser 'Kerr's cur' and a cur, my dictionary tells me, is a type of dog, a worthless or snappy dog. No love lost in politics. As for Kerr himself, Whitlam proclaimed that 'Nothing will save the Governor General,' but nothing was to save Whitlam who was soundly defeated at the election held in 1975. Fraser became

Prime Minister and as for Sir John Kerr, he went to the races, the horse races, not the dogs.

FRASER ISLAND, EASTER ISLAND AND MALCOLM FRASER.

Fraser, a huge man the cartoonists drew as an Easter Island stone figure, was and still is a controversial figure in Australian history. Like all of us, he was a person with one foot in the past and one foot in the present. During his time in office, Fraser had stopped sand mining on Fraser Island (no relation) and he had ended the whaling industry in Australia. He wouldn't stop the construction of the Franklin Dam in Tasmania, however, as he considered that to be a matter for the Tasmanians. The period of his government also saw the first large-scale migration from Asia with 200,000 migrants, including 55,000 Vietnamese, arriving from Asia between 1975 and 1982.

What happened to Fraser? As Liberal leader he won the elections of 1977 and 1980 and then his government was faced with stagflation, the situation when both unemployment and inflation were over 10 per cent. Reprehensible, it was a wonder the Governor General, Sir Ninian Stephens, didn't dismiss him. Not my fault, said Fraser, the recession is a result of global and climatic conditions. Well, he would, wouldn't he? Actually, that sentence should have quotation marks around it. 'Well, he would, wouldn't he?' — Mandy Rice-Davies.

Fraser may have been right, but in politics it is not a matter of being right, it is a matter of providing hope, real or illusory, that you have some answers and the Australian electorate removed his government at the snap election Fraser called in March 1983. Fraser thought he would be opposed by the Labor leader Bill Hayden but at the last minute Hayden was replaced by Robert James Lee Hawke. 'A drover's dog' could have won, Hayden insisted, but 'Kerr's cur' couldn't.

SWIMMING AND SINGING, DIVING AND MIMING.

To make matters worse, this generation had to learn a new national anthem and it wasn't easy for many sportspeople who turned out to be very good at swimming and diving, but not very good at singing, or even miming. In 1974, a poll of 60,000 people undertaken by the Whitlam Labor government voted for 'Advance Australia Fair'. The Fraser Government then had all seven million voters vote and they chose 'Advance Australia Fair' not for our national anthem but for our national song. It received 43 per cent of the vote. The song about the sheep stealer who commits suicide was second on 28 per cent.

Finally in 1984 the national song, 'Advance Australia Fair' was declared the National Anthem. Well, verses one and three became the National Anthem. Verse two about gallant Cook and 'Britannia rules the waves' was dropped as was verse four about England, Scotia and Erin's Isle and verse five was also dispensed with; no references to 'a British soul' was to be in our anthem. Still, now we had an anthem and to inject my own prejudice into the story I quite like it. I like the first two lines, anyway. I can remember them. The rest, I think, is about how we are all going to get rich.

SMALLS STEPS FOR WOMEN.

The 1970 also saw the struggle for equality for women continue. Second wave feminism, it was called, and a lot of grown up female baby boomers were no longer happy to be called 'Baby doll'. Guess the year the following events occurred. The Tram Ride for equal pay when women in Melbourne offered 80 per cent of the fare, the same percentage as they were paid for equal work. The first bank offered a woman a loan without her having to get a male guarantor. The Women's Electoral Lobby advised women to 'Think WEL before you vote'. The first woman advisor to the Prime Minister was appointed, Elizabeth Reid. The first woman Speaker of the House of Representatives was appointed, Joan

Child. Women teachers in Victoria were allowed to join the superannuation fund. The first Australian state passed a *Sex Discrimination Act*. It was South Australia under Don Dunstan. The first woman led an Australian political party. It was Janine Haines and she led the Democrats. So a lot of important milestones were achieved in the 1970s. A lot weren't.

IMPORTANT KILOMETRESTONES IN THE FIELD OF MEASUREMENT.

'Milestone' is probably the wrong word to use as in 1970 the *Metric Conversion Act* was passed and Australia commenced the change to metric units. Took them long enough. In the Parliament in 1901 it was moved that Australia consider adopting the metric system. The National Measurement Institute (NMI) website sets it all out beautifully. It states that in 1988 all remaining imperial units were withdrawn from general legal use. They cannot change language, however. Some older people just will not give an inch, or a foot, or a yard, or a mile, on this point. Indeed the NMI itself lists the steps taken to metric measurement under the heading, 'Important Milestones'. Fair enough, important kilometrestones will never catch on.

As always, the decade ended with work done and work to be done. The eighties had its work cut out for it but it had a whole

90

ten years to solve inflation, unemployment, establish full equality for all Australian citizens, and to deal with emerging issues such as the environment. Plenty of time for the baby boomers, or should they now be called the middle-aged boomers, to solve the problems before they were replaced by their own children, Generation X.

P.S. Answers to the questions in 'Small Steps for Women'.

1970, 1971, 1972, 1973, 1974, 1975, 1976, 1977.

Trends in the Trendy Eighties.

The Ninth 'Decade'.
1983-1996.

The eighties were trendy, at least they were in the eighties when power dressing with shoulder pads replaced the mismatched skirt and sweater for the young upwardly mobile female professional. The eighties also had dinky's, double income no kids yet, and tweenies replaced children. These were all advertising terms designed to get the hard-working, hard-playing people of the eighties to part with their money even if they hadn't earnt any at the time. This was the age of the credit card, an invention which neatly sums up both the optimism and the foolishness of this decade. However, in 1990 the eighties suddenly became untrendy; it happens to every decade.

Mount Never Rest.

In Geography some changes occur violently, dramatically, such as a volcano or an earthquake. Other changes occur slowly when the mountains are transported to the sea, grain by grain. Mountains can even gain by gain, year by

year, as imperceptible pressure forces the mountains upwards. Peak 15 or Sagarmatha or Chomolunga was measured at 29,028 feet in 1954 but has been recently re-measured at 29,035 feet or 8,850 metres. Perhaps you know it better as Mt Everest. This may be due to better measuring techniques but Mt Everest is apparently never at rest, it is rising, inching skywards, a few centimetres every year. Mind you, if global warming produces rising seas then Mt Everest will not be so high above sea level. It's a bit of a race, really. China needs to look out as Mt Never Rest is also moving north-east at the rate of 10 cm per year, as is Australia. We share the same tectonic plate.

History is like that. Some events are dramatic and violent, wars and assassinations, for example. Other events occur slowly as little by little, one by one, people change their thinking and their behaviour. It could be argued that the slow changes end up being the most profound and long lasting. It is time for us to examine some of the trends that have sneaked up on us, not the superficial trends of the world of fashion, but the trends that have profound consequences for us as individuals and for our nation.

RELIGIOUS IDENTITY AND BELIEFS.

If pressed, would you describe Australia as a Christian country, a religious country, a faithless country or a secular country? It has been claimed that Australia has always been a very secular society. We are interested in this life, in the here and now, and questions about the purpose of life, about why we are here, are put to one side as unproductive or unanswerable. I live on the Ballarat goldfields and what strikes me is how many churches were built by the miners who, it has to be conceded, were a very worldly bunch. They were after riches in this life, yet they had very strong religious beliefs at the same time. They were both secular and religious people.

In 1948, 95 per cent of Australians said that they believed in God. By 1998, the figure was down to 74 per cent. Church attendance also appears to be slipping as by 1996 only 10 per cent went to church on a given Sunday and the number was down 300,000 on the situation in 1982. I say 'appears to be slipping' as, if the question is changed to church attendance on a monthly basis, the number grew by 21,000. There has also been a change in numbers belonging to particular religious groups, although not as big a change as you might expect. In 1900, 1 per of Australians were non-Christian. The figure is now 5%. Within the Christian faith, there are now fewer Anglicans, Methodists and Presbyterians but more Catholics, Baptists and Pentecostals.

The figures speak for themselves. No, they don't, the meaning of these figures and the causes and consequences of these trends are a matter of interpretation. Does a decline in religion result in a decline in morality? Does it matter that more people claim to be agnostics or atheists? Does it matter that some religious groups in Australia are growing? The long view of history convinces me that this is not a one-way trend. After the events of 9/11, for example, church attendance increased. For some people, the footy or Australian nationalism is enough to give meaning and identity to their lives, but other people will always look for meaning, ultimate meaning, in their lives.

POOR RESULTS.

Every decade produces reports that state that the rich are getting richer and the poor are getting poorer. Every decade also produces reports that state that the poor are getting richer. How can this be? It depends whether you are measuring absolute poverty, lack of basic human necessities such as food and shelter, or whether you are measuring relative poverty, that, is the wealth and income of the poorest people in society compared to the richest. In 1987, Bob Hawke famously said that by 1990, 'No child shall live in poverty', and that came back to haunt him as the total elimination of poverty, even in a wealthy country, proved to be more difficult than he thought. We gave them the money but some parents were irresponsible and wasted it on beer, Hawke explained 20 years later.

'MY WORD IS MY BOND'.

In economic boom times, and the 1980s was a boom time, everyone gets richer, but the rich get seriously richer, obscenely richer. The eighties was a time of financial deregulation and easy credit and so, by the law of increasing returns, passed when Adam was investing in market gardens, the rich became richer. The classic case was Alan Bond. A beer baron was the old-fashioned name for these entrepreneurs, and Bondie was that and a whole lot more. Media tycoon, founder of a university, national hero when he bankrolled the syndicate that brought home the America's Cup and art connoisseur when three months after the 1987 stock market crash, he bought Van Gogh's 'Blue Irises' for a cool $49 million. Unfortunately, there was a little bit of unpleasantness when he sold it on and diverted the money into a public company. Three years worth of unpleasantness at one of Her Majesty's penal institutions.

AND THE POOR DON'T HAVE CHILDREN.

Population changes in Australia are slow but dramatic in their impact. Between 1980 and 1990 the population increased from 14.7 million to 17.1 million. It is now over 21 million and it is likely to grow by 50 per cent by 2050. With smaller family size, it has been migration that has fueled the increase. Is this a good thing? Oh yes, it is producing a multicultural society, diverse and therefore interesting and stimulating to live in. Migrants also help produce the wealth of the country, and fill job vacancies and that helps reduce inflation.

LOOKING AFTER THOSE WHO LOOKED AFTER YOU BEFORE.

Migrants also tend to be younger and the young will be needed to look after our aging baby boomers. It is ridiculous to talk about old baby boomers, we should call them the retirement boomers, or simply old boomers. In 1900 half the Australian population was more than 22.5 years and by 1987 the figure was 31.3 years, and by 2007 that figure had risen to 36.4 years. The other half was under the median age. In 2006, 3154 Australians had made it to 100 and as this is the fastest growing segment of the Australian population, the Queen will soon be running out of congratulatory telegrams. Or do you now receive an email? Do the elderly need looking after? We will look after ourselves, thank you, say 40 per cent of the centenarians who live independently at home. Good on 'em, but a little bit of 'looking after' is probably required.

On the other hand, recent arrivals tend to live in the big cities and this drives up house prices and puts pressure on infrastructure such as roads and public facilities such as schools, hospitals and public transport. The state of our land and our rivers also makes one wonder what is the carrying capacity of Australia. Of course there are solutions to these problems but we have already seen that solutions usually create a new set of problems. We could all become vegetarians, that will take the pressure off our land and enable us to fit in at least 100 million. It would be a very popular policy as well, with cows, sheep and pigs.

DEBATE LEFT TO THE RIGHT.

Population growth is also going to make it very, very difficult for Australia to reduce greenhouse gas emissions by 60 per cent by

2050. Australians are heavy producers of carbon dioxide, CO_2, at around 27 tonnes per person compared to the Chinese of 3.9 tonnes per person. By 2050, the government wants Australia to reduce carbon emissions from 491 million tonnes to 196 million tonnes. We will be emitting 800 million tonnes if our population continues to grow, says Birrell. No, 'the Government's cuts could be met regardless of rising population with the broad-scale adoption of renewable energy,' says the Climate Institute. (*Sydney Morning Herald* 23/07/2008) 'Additional people, living at our high energy and resource intensive lifestyles means severe demands on an already stressed environment'. (Birrell 2007) Houston, we have a problem, at the very least we have an issue that needs discussion.

It is weird that there is so little public debate on the crucial issue of Australia's population policy. It is more than weird, it is dangerous. When both major political parties agree to agree on an issue, they shut down the real debate and continue with a pretend debate. So what's dangerous about that, surely it shows a national consensus? It is dangerous as it enables others to take up the debate and so we have Pauline Hanson. If policies such as population and migration levels are not discussed by the Left and the Right, then these issues are left to the Right, the extreme Right. Democracy abhors a vacuum, in the long run the electorate will not tolerate it.

LAND RIGHTS.

By 1992, terra nullius, or the doctrine of the empty land, was finally torn up in the Mabo decision made by the High Court. This decision did not come out of the blue but was the culmination of decades of struggle and a decade of gains. In 1966, the Gurindji, led by Vincent Lingiari, went on strike and walked off the Wave Hill cattle station. Ten years later they won a lease on their land and Lord Vesty gave them 90 square kilometres of additional land near Wave Hill. From little things big things do grow. Now known as Dagaragu, it is the first Aboriginal owned and managed cattle station in Australia.

The 500 million-year-old rock which is Uluru (Ayers Rock) also passed to Aboriginal ownership in 1985. This huge sedimentary rock has a perimeter of 8.8 km and presents a smooth appearance to the world as sheets of rock have peeled off as a result of heating and cooling. The process is called spalling. It's really a big onion, a very big onion. The Anangu people had voiced their concerns from 1971 on that the area was under pressure from pastoralism, mining and tourism. It still is under pressure from tourism as by 2003 more than 400,000 people were visiting the rock each year. This compares with 1.5 million visitors to the Grampians in Victoria and over three million to the Kosciuszko National Park. Uluru is a very long way from population centres. One hopes, however, that it is also receiving benefits from tourism, now that it is managed by the traditional and legal owners of the land in conjunction with the Commonwealth Government.

Galloping Inflation Halted.

What happened to the economic, political problems of the last chapter? Did inflation and unemployment just become accepted by the public? Perhaps these problems just went away. No, something even more extraordinary happened. Politicians solved them, well, the main problem of inflation, anyway. Politicians tend to claim credit for the good times and, as we have seen, tend to deny responsibility for the bad times, but at times they do get it right and we all benefit. I know it is unfashionable to say such a thing in Australia but the truth is the truth.

When Hawke won power, inflation was galloping at 11 per cent and 10 years later it was at 1 per cent which could be called toddling inflation or who-cares inflation. This could be another King Canute job, that is, it was nothing to do with Bob Hawke, he just happened to be there at the time. That's not the consensus among most economists. They accept that the prices–income accord implemented by the Hawke Government played a key role in deflating inflation. What he did was to get the unions to moderate their wage demands in return for government concessions on taxation or other benefits. Wage growth slowed down which meant that price increases slowed down; he had broken the wage–price spiral.

BUT WAIT, THERE IS MORE CHANGE.

In 1986, our foreign debt reached $78 billion. The current account deficit was 6.1 per cent of our nations national product. Now, by the way, it is 6.9 per cent but if you have the money to pay off your debt then debt is not a problem. In 1986 we were living beyond our means, we were buying more than we were selling. We will have to make additional changes, said Paul Keating, the Treasurer, otherwise we will not have as much treasure, we will become a banana republic.

For 100 years the Labor movement had focused on the question of the distribution of wealth in this country. Keating now said we must focus our attention on how we produce the wealth in the first place. Be internationally competitive, be efficient, or be poor, was his message. What Keating did was to reverse the decision of our founding fathers and dismantle the trade barriers, the tariffs, that had protected, cocooned Australia for so long. He allowed the Australian dollar to 'float' and so he opened up our economy to the world. Australian factories, farms and mines had to either put up or shut up and that was what they did. Some shut up and others put up their productivity and became exporters to the world.

YES. WE HAVE NO BANANA REPUBLIC.

However, in the recession of 1992, unemployment took off. It was at 9.6 per cent in 1984 and after getting down to under 6 per cent in 1990, it went back to more than 10 per cent by 1992 in 'the recession we had to have'. Painful it was for many working families as many industries took off for the north and left Australia. They went offshore and they took the jobs with them. Keating, however, had taken the steps that allowed Australia to avoid becoming a debt-ridden basket-case of a nation, a banana republic. He did fail to deliver on the Republic but that is another story.

Against the odds, Keating won the sweet electoral victory of 1992 but not the next one, that one was to be the first Howard victory in 1996. Howard inherited all that Hawke and Keating had done, an outward looking economy ready to benefit from globalisation. Howard also inherited all that hadn't been done. In 1996, the unemployment rate was 9.2 per cent. Youth unemployment was 15.7 per cent.

Mr. Howard, Mr. Rudd and You.

The Tenth 'Decade'. 1996-2009.

You are included in the title of this chapter as you are as important as the next person in democratic Australia. We aggressively, at times offensively, believe in equality. We have never tipped our hat to our 'betters' as we do not believe they exist, nor do we 'tip' for service as we believe that people should stand up for themselves and not 'beg' for a top-up. Furthermore, you are included as this is the only chapter in which I can guarantee you were alive at the time, so I thought you would expect to be in the title. I could have been in chapter five.

Unexpected Achievements.

If John Howard had been asked on the night he won the election in 1996, 'What is the main thing that you hope to achieve, the main thing you hope to be remembered for?', do you think he would have said gun control? No, neither do I, but it could well be true. Nor do I think he would have said that it would be the response of his government to a tsunami that killed thousands in Aceh and elsewhere on Boxing Day 2004, but again it could be so. And as for his most famous speech, I doubt whether he would have thought he would have to give a memorial speech over the deaths of 88 Australians killed by religious fanatics in Bali on the 12ᵗʰ of October 2002. The world is indeed an unpredictable place. In the future some issues will still be with us as they are humankind's never-ending concerns, some trends will continue, some will end or be reversed and some totally unforeseen events will shock and test our politicians and our nation. Mr Rudd can expect the unexpected.

THE WAR ON TERROR OR THE SO-CALLED 'WAR ON TERROR'.

Under Kevin Rudd, Australian troops are now in Afghanistan and lots of other dangerous places as well. Under John Howard they were also in Iraq. Has there been an Australian Prime Minister who has not sent Australian troops overseas to a war? Of course, many of the wars are undeclared and many operations are now called 'policing' but essentially they are the use of military force applied at great risk to the lives of our servicemen and women.

The Iraq War divided Australians and many saw it as a repeat of the mistakes of Vietnam. John Howard, often accused of being a populist politician, stuck with this unpopular war as he believed we are at war with terrorists who wish to establish and maintain a tyranny, secular (Iraq) or religious (Afghanistan) that ultimately threatens the democratic world. To his opponents, the War on Terror is the so called 'War on Terror'. Inverted commas or 'so called' is used to hint that they suspect other, less noble, motives. As for the consequences of the Iraq War, we wait. Will Iraq, the Middle East and the World be a better place because of the war in Iraq? It largely depends on whether the war has moved Iraq towards democracy or chaos.

IMMEASURABLE MEASURABLE PROGRESS.

It is time to issue Australia its end of century report card. The Australian Bureau of Statistics (ABS) does just that with its wonderfully titled 'Measures of Australia's Progress'. What a heading! It is a heading that could have been used in 1900 or 1950 or in the year 2008. Apart from the heavy consumption of alcohol, it seems the belief in Progress is the one constant in our story. We are true believers in Australia as a lucky country and with the right decisions and good management we believe we can make life on this continent even better. Politicians, captains of industry, newspaper editors, city councillors, all classes, all faiths and private members of the local Progress Association, all believe in Progress. These up-to-date figures from the Bureau, by the way, were released at 11.30am (Canberra Time) on the 17th May, 2008. What is Canberra Time? Many Australians have suspected that Canberra was not in the same time zone as the rest of us, and now they admit it.

Progress for Progressive Individuals.

'All three indicators for individuals suggest progress during the last decade'. (ABS 2008) The indicators indicate we are living longer, are better educated and fewer of us are unemployed. Life expectancy is now 83 for women and 79 for men. The percentage with a non-school qualification, post-school would be a better term, has increased from 46 per cent to 59 per cent in the decade. The unemployment rate has been lowered from 8.3 per cent in 1996 to 4.4 per cent in 2007. The Bureau asserts that paid work is a good thing as it 'contributes to a person's sense of identity and self-esteem'. It also contributes to their income! Labor supporters claim that all this is due to circumstances beyond Howard's control. But I gave Hawke and Keating credit for deflating inflation, so I give Howard the credit for nearly halving unemployment. Living longer, better educated and fewer unemployed, so why say that this 'suggests' progress? Be bold, it is Progress with a capital P!

Measurable Economic Progress.

Our real net wealth per person grew, and we were not only healthier, we were wealthier. The 1990s were to be very good years, with another mining boom. Off went the coal and iron and bauxite to China and India and Japan and back came the cars and the air conditioners and huge televisions for our homes. Yes, we were richer as our income grew by 2.9 per cent per year over the last ten years. Even working families in the lower income group saw their income grow by 31 per cent over the ten years. And $556 billion was invested in homes which the Bureau points out, quite profoundly, is a good thing as 'Housing provides people with shelter, security and privacy'. We all need somewhere to change, you know.

UNMEASURABLE COMMUNITY PROGRESS.

Healthier? Yes. Wealthier? Yes. Wiser? Unmeasurable. Happier? What says the Happiness Index? Unfortunately, Australia doesn't have one; Bhutan does so perhaps we can learn from them although Wikipedia sadly informs us that, 'There is no exact quantitative definition of Gross National Happiness'. Are we less likely to kill each other, rob each other and more likely to help each other? More volunteer work was done, and with an aging population there were plenty of elderly Australians who need to be helped across the road and back again as required. It would be awful to leave them stranded on the other side. Personal crime increased, however, but household crime fell. So, as you are more likely to be mugged walking down the street, but less likely to have your television stolen, you can watch the report of the bashing on your own television as soon as you recover.

How healthy is our democracy? In 1988, 6 per cent of Members of the House of Representatives were women and in 2008 the figure was 27 per cent. Wonderfully high or shockingly low? In 2008, 80 per cent of 18–25 year olds eligible to vote were actually enrolled. Wonderfully high or shockingly low? What we can and should boast about is that as a nation we can change government without anyone getting killed and that is a very rare occurrence in the long, sad history of humankind. It happens regularly in Australia. It happened again in 2007.

DOUBTS ABOUT DROUGHTS AND FLOODING RAINS.

No-one doubts that we have a drought but has the drought something to do with our own activity, the activity that generates our wealth and power? Australia has had droughts before, long severe droughts at that. Ironically, this is where we came in as The Federation Drought of 1895–1902 was our most severe one before this current drought. Fools learn by their own experience, wise people learn by other people's experience, from History, in other words. So, as we are now aware of the fact that we live in the driest continent, we will value and use our scarce water resources more carefully. Of course we will, won't we, even if it costs us a little, or a bit, or a lot? Fortunately, as a rich country we will have the money to tackle climate change in this country. Ironically, we will get the money from our sale of coal to China.

Bigger is still better, however. Melbourne is outgrowing Sydney. Hurrah! Ballarat reaches 100,000. Hurrah! We cannot let go of our belief in development. We still speak of development but now it is 'sustainable development'. Can the growth of the Australian suburbs be sustained? Can car use be sustained? Can growth in energy consumption for our McMansions be sustained? Can the Murray–Darling River system be sustained as our food bowl, as a healthy river and as a source of water to support growing urban cities? I think fewer Australians would now answer these questions with the naïve optimism of the 1900s. There is nothing wrong with doubt. Its called thinking, and knowledge comes from doubt.

A Sorry Affair.

Doubts and disappointment are also evident in the crucial area of Aboriginal policy. The Parliament has said sorry for the stolen generation, the Aboriginal flag flies everywhere, but dignity and a respected role in modern Australia eludes many Aboriginal people. The figures cannot be denied or ignored. Aboriginal life expectancy is 17 years less than the life expectancy of other Australians. Substance abuse, crime and incarceration rates are far too high. Aboriginal housing, income and employment are also a national disgrace. What is the situation now for the Anangu at Uluru and at the Dagaragu cattle station? What is to be done? What is the advice of Aboriginal leaders such as Noel Pearson, Pat Dobson, Warren Mundine and Professor Roger Thomas?

The Bottom Line.

If you are a Labor supporter your summary to be written at the bottom of Australia's report card would be, 'Could do better'. If you are a Greens supporter the bottom line would be, 'Could do a lot better'. If you are a Liberal supporter your bottom line would be, 'Has done very well'. If you are an Independent your bottom line answer will be long and complex and subtle and slightly confused and contradictory. Fortunately, the summary report cannot say, 'This country will be required to repeat the century'. We are, however, returning to rethink many of the issues of 1900.

Today, we are 'having a stab at' the major issues of our times. They are the very same issues addressed by the Edwardians. They also grappled with questions about population and migration and equity and development, defence and Aboriginal rights. Are we coming up with better answers?

EPILOGUE

We have arrived at the beginning of the future. At this point it must be said that history 'ends'. Of course, as long as there are humans, history will never end, but I can write no more, no evidence being available.

Again, I apologise for leaving out your ancestors and indeed for leaving out your good self. I have the same excuse as last time, no room.

So in summary, what are the main points? Truth is stranger than fiction, that is my thesis, and I stick to that simple point. The human story is seriously weird.

As for the crucial lessons of History, well, I am sorry but 'Ancora Imparo' – I am still learning. I am still working on it. I wouldn't wait for me to work it out. Indeed, the whole point is that you should work it out yourself. Continue to read and think. Get on with it.

But as far as this book is concerned, I end by flagrantly copying, by way of a compliment, the ending of the greatest history book ever written. I leave you to work out the name of that book.

We have arrived at the present. So finally History comes to a .

Bibliography

- Adam-Smith, Patsy *Australian women at war.* Nelson 1984.
- Anderson, Hugh *Australia in the Depression.* Hill of Content 1972.
- Bagley, W. O. 'Coroner's Enquiry into the Sunshine Railway Disaster'. Melbourne 1909.
- Blainey, Geoffrey *Black Kettle and Full Moon.* Viking 2003.
- Boyd, Robin *The Australian Ugliness.* Penguin 1963.
- Caulfield, Michael *The Vietnam Years.* Hachette Australia. 2007.
- Cathcart, M. and K. Darian-Smith *Stirring Australian Speeches.* Melbourne University Press 2004.
- Carlyon, Les *The Great War.* Macmillan 2006.
- Cole, E. W. *A White Australia Impossible, and for very important reasons Undesirable.* EW Cole Book Arcade 1902.
- Crisp, L. F. *Ben Chifley.* Longmans 1961.
- Crowley, F. K. *A New History of Australia.* Heinemann 1974.
- Daly, Fred *From Curtin to Kerr.* Sun Books 1977.
- Downey, L. A *Pig-Raising in Australia.* Angus and Robertson 1951.
- Galbraith, John Kenneth *The Great Crash 1929.* Penguin Books 1975.
- Gammage, Bill *The Broken Years. Australian Soldiers in the Great War.* Penguin 1975.
- Hardy, Frank *It's Moments Like These….* Gold Star 1972.
- Hazlehurst, Cameron *Menzies Observed.* Allen and Unwin 1975.
- Hawke, Bob *The Hawke Memoirs.* Heinemann 1994.
- Herbert, Xavier *Poor Fellow My Country.* Collins 1975.
- Hirst, John *Australia's Democracy. A short history.* Allen and Unwin 2002.
- Hirst, John *Sense and Nonsense in Australian History.* Black Inc Agenda 2006.
- Inson, G. and R. Ward *The Glorious Years.* Jacaranda 1971.

- Keesing, Nancy The White Chrysanthemum, Angus and Robertson 1972.
- Lines, William Taming the Great South Land. Allen and Unwin 1991.
- Low, David The Billy Book. Hughes Abroad. NSW Bookstall 1918.
- Lowenstein, Wendy Weevils in the Flour. Hyland House 1978.
- McKernon, Michael Drought: the red marauder. Allen and Unwin 2005.
- Marshall, Jock and Russell Drysdale Journey among Men.
  Hodder and Stoughton 1962.
- Monash, Sir John The Australian Victories in France in 1918. Lothian 1920.
- van Oudtshoorn, Nic 'Victoria. History as it Happened'.
  Herald and Weekly Times. 1986.
- Summers, Anne Damned Whores and God's Police. Penguin 1975.
- Stanley, Dr Peter 'Was there a Battle for Australia?'
- Australian War Memorial Anniversary Oration 10 November 2006.
- Wynn-Jones, Michael The Cartoon History of Britain. Tom Stacey 1971.
- Year Book Commonwealth of Australia No 26, 1933.